DATE DUE

9.02 0 8.96			
		Printed in USA	

HIGHSMITH #45230

THE CO-OP BRIDGE

Cynthia Parsons

With: William J. Cirone
John R. Coleman

Woodbridge / *Santa Barbara, California 93160*

Parsons, Cynthia.

The co-op bridge /

First edition.

Published and distributed by

Woodbridge Press Publishing Company
Post Office Box 6189
Santa Barbara, California 93160

Copyright © 1991 by Cynthia Parsons.

Manufactured in the United States of America.
Distributed simultaneously in the United States and Canada.

Library of Congress Cataloging-in-Publication Data:

Parsons, Cynthia.
 The Co-op Bridge / Cynthia Parsons : with William J. Cirone,
John R. Coleman. — 1st ed.
 ISBN 0-88007-186-9 : $7.95
  1. Education, Cooperative— United States. 2. Student Service— United
States. I. Cirone, William J. II. Coleman, John R. III. Title.
LB1029.C6P275   1990
370.19'31— dc20   90-15482
                                                          CIP

Cover design by Carol Krieger.
Typeset by Lasertype Publishing, Chester, Vermont.
Printed by Patterson Press, Benton Harbor, Michigan.

Quantity purchases: Individuals or organizations wishing to distribute this
book in quantity may request special terms from the publisher.

DEDICATION

For Douglas Brutsché
A very special
friend

Table of Contents

Prelude
William J. Cirone

I've never met Cynthia Parsons. Our linkages have occurred only through our writings -- she through hers and I through mine, and together through our correspondence. Our bridge to each other has been crafted upon a shared vision of the future and how best to get there.

Still, I am now embarrassed to say, I was hesitant to write this prelude...until reading "The Co-op Bridge." Then, without a second thought, I felt privileged that she had extended the invitation. For in these pages, Cynthia articulates clearly, persuasively, irrefutably, the argument for what she terms "cooperative learning" as a bridge for young people from the world of school to the world of work.

And it seems absolutely illogical -- perhaps even irresponsible -- that we have not been practicing cooperative learning everywhere, all along.

I said that Cynthia and I share a vision of the future for our young people. It's one I know most people share: Children growing up in good health, well nourished, with adequate clothing, and a zest for learning and living. With a spark inside that makes them want to share their talents with those less fortunate, to work for the good of the order, just because it's the right thing to do.

Free of fear, free of abuse, free of drugs, free of prejudice. Free to reach beyond their circumstances, whatever those might be, and to join a society that welcomes their contributions on the job, in the community, and in the voting booth.

Unfortunately, as we all know, this is not always the case. The Children's Defense Fund (CDF) paints a different portrait of the conditions of children in America. According to CDF statistics, on a typical day in the United States, some 16,833 women get pregnant, and 2,740 of them are teenagers. That's every day.

On that same typical day, 69 babies die before reaching their one-month birthday, 27 children die because of poverty, nine children die from guns, and six teens commit suicide. More than 7,700 teens become sexually active every day, according to the CDF figures, and 623 teens get syphilis or gonorrhea. We do not yet know how many contract AIDS.

I believe to my core that we can help bring about a change and reverse these trends. Cooperative learning may well be the critical component that tips the balance for the vast majority of at-risk young people, by giving them purpose, hope, skills, and perhaps more important, a vision of the future that shifts their focus from today to tomorrow, and causes them to defer gratification and work toward a goal that is as rewarding as it is attainable.

While cooperative learning is a notion that has been around a long time, nationally only about 10 percent of our student participate in such a program. In The Co-op Bridge, Cynthia Parsons proposes that ALL students -- kindergarten through college, but most particularly secondary students -- be required to take cooperative education. *If her proposal were implemented, I believe it could become the most far-reaching and important educational reform of the century.*

Cynthia argues that cooperative education is not in competition for limited and valuable time with other course offerings. Rather, it is a hands-on method of teaching all courses, including fundamental literacy skills.

I agree. I've always found that a learn-by-doing approach to teaching pumps relevancy into subject-matter. It is in the best John Dewey tradition of teaching. Further, adolescents today need more than ever to be connected in a meaningful way to their community. They need to feel needed and involved. Cooperative learning can be a critical bridge to connecting our youngsters with their community. Yet it is not an end in itself. "Put liberal-arts first," Cynthia insists. "Co-op ed second."

The trick is to avoid seeing cooperative learning as an isolated, free-standing program. As Cynthia points out, in good cooperative learning programs, textbook learning is reinforced by the work/service experience. Cooperative education can be viewed as an internship or apprenticeship. The key to making this happen is careful planning, supervision, dialogue, and counseling. The Co-op Bridge *provides the context, concept, and implementation strategies. It demonstrates that K-12 educators cannot make this happen alone. Employers must be involved, and teacher training programs must take steps to prepare classroom practitioners.*

As Cynthia points out, 50 years ago nearly three-fourths of all school-aged children lived in homes with no college graduates and nearly every school teacher and administrator was the first person in a family to have graduated from a four-year college. Because secondary schools wanted to place their top students in college, a bridge was needed to help with the transition. As a result, the college counseling program was born in our high schools.

Colleges wanted the counselors because it gave them a single contact point and made their jobs easier. Teacher training departments recognized the importance and growth potential of this school-related job and instituted programs to teach this bridging skill.

Cynthia argues that this bridge from high school to college can be replicated in a bridge from high school to work. Businesses will certainly find co-op ed counselors and programs useful. Eventually, colleges will begin offering courses and majors related to cooperative education.

Why bother? As Cynthia explains, there would be no need if the best and brightest undergraduates were already signing up to major in education. Or if graduates of teaching schools were not involved in the faily _, naif the nation's school children. Or if learning by doing was an inadequate and inappropriate teaching method. Or if secondary school years were not the time when adolescents should learn primary job skills and appropriate workplace behavior. Or if the doing of civic service would not enhance the teaching of civics.

In short, The Co-op Bridge is must reading for all concerned about our educational system, our work force, our at-risk students, our future leaders. Evidence of the need to re-examine our basic approaches surround us: a growing dropout rate, declining participation in our electoral process, and the alarming concern on the part of the private sector about students graduating without the skills and attitudes necessary to be successful in the workplace.

Cooperative learning for all students, carefully conceived and properly implemented, can become the learning-by-doing tool our students so desperately need.

An ancient Chinese proverb states: "Tell me and I remember; involve me and I understand."

William J. Cirone is Santa Barbara County, California, Superintendent of Schools; president of the National Community Education Association; board member of the national IMPACT II teacher recognition and support program; and widely known advocate for community service and civic literacy programs.

Introduction

It's only fair that I should start this book with a hearty acknowledgment of and praise for The William T. Grant Foundation Commission on Work, Family and Citizenship. For some dozen years, I'd been saying I would write about "cooperative education," but it wasn't until Samuel Halperin, the commission's study director, engaged me to write a paper on cooperative education for their <u>Youth and America's Future</u> project that I actually did the writing I had procrastinated about for so many years.

After what I hoped would be my final draft was circulated among vocational, work-study, cooperative education, and liberal-arts educationists, I was asked to do a complete re-write. I read the thoughtful critiques -- but disagreed rather fundamentally. I met with Dennis Gray and David Lynn, and listened carefully to their substantive arguments, but quite unpersuaded, I did the re-write, kept to my basic thesis, and they kept to their criticisms.

In time, my paper was printed, bound, and distributed by the commission, along with critical commentaries from Roy L. Wooldridge, Morgan V. Lewis, as well as Lynn & Gray.

I believe I do them no disservice when I state that their fundamental disagreement with my paper, "The Bridge:

Cooperative Education for All High School Students," is the fact that I think all secondary schools should guide and supervise on-the-job training (in non-profit, civic, and free-enterprise settings) for all students.

Our communities have three jobs to do for all children in the 10 years in which schooling is compulsory: Literacy for all capable of understanding the 3 R's; preparation for full-time work assignments in job settings; a fundamental understanding of both the rights and responsibilities inherent in our political democracy.

I believe that the best way to teach fundamental literacy skills is to combine those academic skills with worthwhile activities. I believe this is true even for those rare students whose photographic memory abilities make them appear to be learning with understanding when, often, the learning is only superficial.

We've made some serious mistakes not only in the way we teach students and prepare future teachers, but in the placement of our school buildings and in their size. Small is better.

Schools placed within the community are essential in order that we may have community schools.

Let me quote from a commentary on school restructuring by Anthony Doria, a founder of the Vermont Law School.

"Once, the school was the center of community life. Today we build free-standing schools, municipal buildings, senior citizen centers, etc. thereby multiplying our expenses even as we dilute and divide our resources.

"Picture if you can a multipurpose community building, where parents and taxpayers go to transact business, and in the process mingle with students and teachers; where students learn government and business by working at it in the town clerk's and treasurer's office, rather than out of textbooks; where [the] elderly...share with youngsters their vast wealth of experience and in turn draw companionship and a sense of being needed. I dare say, children sharing a cafeteria table with a senior citizen could learn something at least as valuable during lunch as in a classroom."

Now, let me amend Mr. Doria. I would not say that students should learn government and business "by working at it in the town clerk's and treasurer's office, rather than out of textbooks;" no, I would say that students should learn government and business by working at it in the town clerk's and treasurer's office as well as out of their textbooks. Or, as a complement to what they learn in their textbooks. Or, integrated with their classroom reading and discussion.

But I couldn't agree more with Mr. Doria that we need to stop building free-standing schools; need to stop isolating students from their community; that we need to meld school and community as one.

I abhor "shopping mall" high schools.
I abhor "tracked" schools.
I abhor "self-contained" classrooms.
I abhor "graded" schools.
I abhor "isolated" countryside schools.

3

I am, of course, tempted to "rattle on" writing about all the changes schools should make to "be what they should be." But I am going to be careful; I shall stick to my subject.

We need to build bridges for all our students by integrating academics and work experience in such compelling ways that <u>all</u> students will leave our schools not only knowing how to read and write, but how to fill a job slot in our free-enterprise and/or public-service economy.

There are those who want our schools to concentrate on a rich liberal-arts type curriculum, and who eschew any distraction with job skills and job preparation. They argue that 10 years of schooling is hardly enough for the liberal-arts needs of our nation's children, and that work skills and jobs rightfully belong <u>after</u> the fundamental schooling years.

I don't disagree with them; I want every student to have a liberal, not a vocational junior and senior high school experience.

What I do argue is that the integration of classical learning with work-place decisions -- not full-time jobs, but part-time work experiences -- enhances the academics while preparing students for productive employment. I trust that the remainder of this volume will not only clarify this point, but make it irrefutable.

There are those who argue that specific skill training should be undertaken only by a few students...somehow early in their school experience determined by whether they have such an aptitude. And those who maintain that only about one of every ten of these students should "do" cooperative education;

4

that is, integrate academics and vocational training. For the other ninety percent, little effort is made to integrate what's taught in the academic classes with what's taught in the vocational school shops.

There are those who agree with the position espoused by some labor unions, that youngsters should not be given on-the-job training because if there is a job to do, it should be done by a union worker. Similarly, there are those who argue civil service jobs should be done only by qualified civil servants.

And there are those who say that the business, non-profit, and civil service jobs in a community should be done only by adults, and that supervising student interns is not a "proper" work assignment.

But co-op ed isn't supposed to be full-time adult employment. It is, instead, what used to be called an "apprenticeship," and today is often referred to as an "internship."

If business, industry, the state and federal civil service, and the armed forces are to be believed, they receive young adults -- many of whom have completed 12 years of schooling -- who require immediate training. Training, these employers argue, which the young entry-level workers should have received in school. Not just work habits, or basic job skills, but basic literacy. That being the case, it would seem that these future employers would be more than a little interested in all students receiving co-op ed assignments while still in school, hence providing them with better-skilled and better academically-educated entry-level employees.

But my reasons for espousing co-op ed are not driven solely by the demands of the market place. I espouse co-op ed because it is "learning by doing." I espouse co-op ed because it engages young people in community needs, preparing them to be problem-solvers, light-givers, not adolescents of darkness and depression.

I herald co-op ed because many of our finest teachers are not full-time in a classroom, but are found in supervisory and management positions throughout our service and business industries.

I want co-op ed offered to every secondary-level pupil because we must do everything we can -- all of us together -- to shorten that period of youthful immaturity known as "adolescence."

No other society in the history of mankind has so lengthened adolescence as has the United States since the close of WWIi. An economist would put it: No other society could have afforded to have adulthood so delayed.

We've been rightly called a "throw-away" society. And we've thrown away our children by rising numbers. What does the Grant Commission call them? "The Forgotten Half."

We've given up on just about one of every two pupils in our public schools; and done so early in their 10-year conscription period. Furthermore, we have built no bridge between childishness and adult commitment for more than half of our upcoming citizens. We've built no bridge for those who have dropped out, or been expelled. We've built no bridge for those whose inadequate literacy skills make them unemployable.

And I'd be the first to say that just giving marginal youngsters work experience will not dissolve "the forgotten half." We've got to do a lot more than add co-op ed to a crowded syllabus. But I'm also glad to be one of those who say that co-op ed is a "must" for every adolescent; a missing ingredient between puberty and maturity.

If you agree with me, I suppose you'll go ahead and read the rest of this book; at least those chapters which look interesting to you.

If you don't agree with me, particularly if you are a parent or guardian, I plead with you to browse through the chapters which follow. If you <u>do</u> become persuaded that I do have a point, and that every youngster in every school should have the opportunity for co-op ed, then it will take massive pressure on your part to restructure the offerings in your local school district so that co-op ed is included.

Sorry to say, less than 10 percent of the secondary schools nationwide -- as I write this in my one-room schoolhouse home located on the side of the road in rural Vermont -- have active co-op ed programs in place. An enormous number of teachers and school administrators never did co-op ed when they were in school, and so it does not seem "natural" to them to offer it to youngsters who would thrive under such active learning.

Furthermore, very very sorry to say, none of the colleges or universities training would-be teachers teach their students how to organize, supervise, document, and evaluate co-op ed.

The author of this book -- The Co-op Bridge -- will, in the pages which follow, do her utmost to explain not only why all schools should offer co-op ed, but how they should do so, and what enormous benefits come from so doing.

Where <u>The Co-op Bridge</u> fails to persuade, the fault, good reader, is in the writer, not the concept. After all, it's my academic understanding together with my work-place activity -- my own cooperative education -- which has produced this book.

Cynthia Parsons
The Gassetts Schoolhouse
Chester, Vermont
August 1990

CHAPTER ONE
What is cooperative education?

Ideally, co-op ed is schooling which fuses or integrates academics with job skills. [Running errands and doing research for a town lawyer under the joint supervision of the lawyer, and the social studies and English teachers.]

It's not work-study; i.e. if the work is unrelated to the study. [Working a fast-food counter without reference to any academic coursework.] Such work-study could become co-op ed if the work experience was jointly supervised and evaluated by academic teachers as well as on-the-job supervisors. And if the academic teachers made use of the fast-food experience in English, science, math, and social studies coursework.

It's not traditional voc ed; particularly if the work experience is done in a school "shop." [Small engine repair unconnected with lessons in English composition, physics, mathematics, or social studies classes.] But even with on-site shop experience, vocational training in specific skills such as engine repair, welding, electronics, etc., could well be turned into co-op ed by integrating the academic coursework with the shop work.

There is a school which offers to fix small engines for any handicapped or senior citizen. The work is done in the school shop. Unless this shop is operated along the management style of a real repair shop, most co-op ed purists would not consider this as cooperative education. For them, "cooperative" means just that -- two agencies working together: a business and a school.

But let's put that concern aside for a few paragraphs. Should the English teacher help students who take this shop course to write, edit, and produce public-access radio scripts advertising the small engine repair service, we see what the "label" co-op ed begins to mean. The same, or another English teacher, might well expect the required oral presentations made by these shop students to be based on what they are doing and learning in the shop, hence enriching both the shop work and skills, and the ability to describe such technical activities.

But we'll need the science teachers whose students take this small-engine repair shop to correlate their science teaching with the students' work experience. And need the math teachers to call for problem-solving strategies using the shop experience. That is, if we're going to fit the above definition of co-op ed.

Let's come back to that first example, to the student working part-time for the town lawyer. We can imagine a clever social studies teacher asking students, as they read about the legislative branch within the government of the United States, to wonder what a town lawyer might have to do. This, by the teacher, in order to make the academic coursework more relevant, and hence better able to be retained in thought by the young students.

But what if the same teacher arranged for each student to put in some job time in their town's public legal system? And what if the teacher used the experiences to make reading and research assignments for the academic coursework?

And what if the students, as part of their final exam for the academic course, had to make an oral presentation explaining one point in the law learned both on-the-job, and through research activities?

And what if the judges evaluating the oral presentation consisted of those who supervised the work experience as well as the social studies and English teachers?

Certainly, English literature courses could include material about the law, as well as legal material itself. Students working in law offices, then, would not only be in the same environment with lawyers, but simultaneously students of law.

Now let's come back to the small-engine repair class. Co-op ed purists argue that job skills should be pursued in actual job settings, not in school shops. Some years ago, when a school district was investigating building and operating a new county vocational school, the automobile shop teacher went to several of the area service stations to ask them what they thought about the school having its own shop area for the students to practice their repair skills.

He was surprised to discover that not one of them agreed with him. All made the point that the best place for a student to learn a skill was in a real shop, where the student would not only be able to get practical training and practice, but would have to meet on-the-job standards.

Hence, most co-op ed teachers would want those students learning to repair small engines to be working in a shop which repaired small engines, getting the same back-up academically, as well as similar opportunities to integrate the skill-learning with the academics, but having to adjust to whatever requirements were in force at the job site.

At the college level, there are even arguments that all co-op ed, to be given college-level credit, must be paid employment, requiring students to fulfill all employee requirements for each hiring situation.

At the junior and senior high school level, compensation for co-op ed is seldom an issue, and almost never a requirement for passage of a course or a high school degree.

The question comes up about schedule when any school begins to explore cooperative education. There would appear to be as many scheduling schemes as schools involved!

Some students are given one day a week to be on-the-job, and have academic classes for only four days. Others must do their work assignments "outside school time." Still others "sandwich" the work experience and the academics mornings and afternoons.

In some cases, the work experience is a full-time activity, maybe taking up the entire length of a marking period, and the remainder of the school year devoted to the necessary related academics.

There has been a growing trend to allow co-op ed for college-bound students only during the final marking period of their senior year. This puts the out-of-school work time after students have been accepted (or have chosen) their college, and often is done as "independent study" under the supervision of one or more academic teachers in conjunction with work-place supervisors.

Often these special work/study (co-op ed) experiences are handled as internships in not-for-profit settings; and are part of the student's community service activity -- all part of being accepted at the college of their choice.

Unfortunately, some schools just allow students to go off and take jobs during this final marking period, without making any work/study connections. Reasons abound for not doing so, generally stemming from lack of staff to supervise and guide.

But let's look at one possible co-op ed assignment. Imagine a student of Spanish in a school district with many immigrant Hispanics. And let's imagine that the student has completed all high school credits, been accepted by a college, and would like, for the final marking period, to tutor adults taking language courses at a local continuing education center.

And let's imagine that the school agrees that students attend no classes, but work a minimum of 30 hours a week at the center. But also to require a final paper describing the experience written in Spanish, translated by the student into English, and graded by both the Spanish and English faculty.

Let's further imagine that the student not only receives help with teaching techniques from the public center staff, but from the school faculty, particularly the foreign language instructors.

That's co-op ed.

Here's a further look at co-op ed in the town of Utopia, U.S.A.

Mary went to high school in a medium-size town. When her guidance counselor first met with her in grade 9, Mary indicated a budding interest in fashion as a possible career path. At the same time, she explained that her family was eager for her to go on to college after high school.

The guidance counselor provided the cooperative education coordinator with Mary's cumulative academic record folder, and alerted her to Mary's interest in merchandising and retailing. Together they worked out a schedule of courses combining college-prep with co-op vocational.

Mary took such courses as: bookkeeping and algebra; accounting and geometry; public speaking and English literature; contemporary American thought and ancient history.

During grades 9 and 10, Mary spent full time in school, and worked intermittently in local retail stores after school, weekends, and holiday periods. The co-op ed teacher helped her get some of the jobs; others she got on her own.

During grades 11 and 12, Mary began a co-op ed schedule which placed her full time in a store for two of her school's four marking periods of 10 weeks each. She worked in one store

14

During grades 11 and 12, Mary began a co-op ed schedule which placed her full time in a store for two of her school's four marking periods of 10 weeks each. She worked in one store during grade 11, and over the following summer. She transferred to another store (sports equipment) for grade 12, as she'd begun to decide on sports fashions as her main interest.

When Mary was not working at either store, she was in school full time, and another co-op ed student from her high school filled the same job slot.

Both Mary and her other "half" (a different student each year) met with 20 other co-op ed pairs in a seminar course to discuss work-related issues throughout the 11th and 12th grade academic years. This seminar received full academic course credit each year, had reading and writing assignments, and was team taught by school staff and representatives of the cooperative businesses.

Mary, tall and lithe, was a varsity basketball player, and with help from her guidance counselor and co-op ed coordinator, arranged her year so that she worked full time for the first and last marking periods, and was a full-time student from the second week in November through the first week in April, during the period her school was involved in basketball competitions.

Mary also was active with the school newspaper and yearbook, and because she worked Saturdays during her co-op terms, she was able to arrange her 40-hour work weeks at the two stores so that she could be at school for those extra-curricular club meetings even during her co-op work terms.

Hernandez attended a large city high school which operated two sessions a day. Since the summer after 10th grade, he was a co-op ed worker/student in a local bank.

That first summer, he didn't do much but run errands. But when the school year started, Hernandez began working in the data processing department, punching in on the clock at 8 A.M., and out at 12 noon weekdays; than arriving at school at 1 P.M., and taking classes until 4 P.M. Besides the required academic courses, he was enrolled in a set of computer workshops or short courses; here he learned to operate a series of increasingly complex business computer systems.

Hernandez was on the track team, and had to do his practice afternoons. And since some track meets pulled him out of class a few days of the year, he had to do "make-up" course work in his free time.

Hernandez, who had asked for the data processing job at the bank, did so because of his interest in and skill with computer technology. His high school had a number of computers and some good computer technicians as teachers. He found that his work at the bank helped him with his computer course work at school.

Willie Mae, in the same year at the same high school as Hernandez, filled the data processing job slot at the bank by starting her work day at 1 P.M., and ending at 5 P.M. Willie

Mae started her school day at 8 A.M., and her last class was over by 11:20 A.M.

She was not scheduled in the same seminar as Hernandez because his met in the afternoon and hers in the morning. But she and Hernandez did have a computer project they were doing together for their Computer II class.

They were using bank rate fluctuations to make predictions based on what they learned on the job, and what they studied with their mathematics teachers.

Willie Mae decided to meet her physical education requirement by joining a local swim club, and with two of her co-workers from the bank, swam three afternoons a week after work.

During his senior year, Hernandez got interested in computer programming, but the bank kept him doing data processing for the entire work period. Because he was quick at the work he was doing at the bank, they invited him to stay on after high school as a full-time employee.

But Hernandez wanted to go on to a city college, and to get a degree in computer programming. The bank compromised, asking him to work full time over the summer and 30 hours a week when he was going to college. They sweetened the proposal by offering to reimburse him for the cost of his tuition for any course he passed with a C+ or better.

Willie Mae, on the other hand, decided not to go on to college after graduation; nor did she apply to the bank for a full-time job. Instead, she took a job in the data processing office of a large department store, where she could stretch her 40-hour

17

week over six days, and be able to augment her earnings with the store discount.

Her co-op ed coordinator helped her find the store job even before she finished the co-op at the bank. This meant she could start the new job as soon as she finished her school course work.

George lived in a rural area, sometimes with his mother, and sometimes with other family relatives. Most of his school years were difficult, and he had to repeat 3rd grade. When he got to the 9th grade, the only job the co-op ed counselor could help him get was one helping the custodian at the high school.

And the only jobs the custodian would give him were cleaning.

George did such a good enough job cleaning up after the first varsity basketball game of the season that the coach went out of his way to praise him; also gave him a free pass for all home games.

The general science teacher backed up George's cleaning job by getting him involved with some of the college-prep chemistry students in some lab work analyzing cleaning agents.

By the time George got to the 11th grade, he and the co-op ed coordinator were able to find him two nighttime cleaning jobs (midnight to 4 A.M.) in a grocery store and a public health clinic. Also the coordinator worked out George's school schedule so that his classes all met in the early afternoon, giving George the mornings to sleep.

He still worked with the school custodians, and when he graduated took a full-time job on the custodial staff at the high school, and immediately took on a young co-op student as a helper.

Anna was enrolled in a large urban high school, had no specific work or academic interests, no hobbies, and joined none of the school's many extra-curricular clubs. Her 9th grade guidance counselor, after Anna said she didn't need or want an after-school job, didn't send her file onto the co-op ed coordinator.

At the close of her 10th grade year, Anna's file was sent automatically to one of the co-op ed counselors who had to set up five appointments before Anna showed up. "No!" Emphatically, she did not want help getting a summer job; she would be "with friends" all summer.

Fall, junior year, the co-op ed counselor made an appointment with Anna after reviewing her cumulative academic folder and finding a scattering of Ds, but mostly Cs. And also finding that Anna was absent several days each month.

"No," definitely, Anna did "not want an outside job. No, working in a clothing store was boring. No, I don't like office work and I can't type. No, I don't like waiting on table, customers are always changing their orders."

Finally they agreed on a job, and Anna was assigned to work in a nearby day-care center starting at noon and ending each day at 6 P.M. First, she was assigned food preparation and clean-up jobs, and not allowed to work directly with either the infants or the toddlers.

But as her work and attendance improved, she discovered she was genuinely interested in playing games with the older toddlers, particularly word games and picture puzzles. Her supervisor told the co-op ed coordinator about Anna's improved "attitude," and suggested that Anna's English teacher should reinforce the word-game interests.

By the late spring of her 11th grade year, Anna took a hand in deciding -- along with her co-op ed coordinator and guidance counselor -- which courses to take her senior year: two English, one in children's literature and one in public speaking; a contemporary history; and an ecology class. These classes met in the mornings; Anna continued her job at the day-care center in the afternoons.

She was enrolled, as well, in a co-op ed seminar along with other seniors working with infants and children in one capacity or another. For her contemporary history class, she, along with two others in her seminar, wrote a paper comparing day care facilities in Scandinavia with those in the United States. Their paper won a school prize.

Utopia!

Mary, Hernandez, Willie Mae, George, and Anna all appear to have dealt with cooperative businesses with no union interference and bosses willing to be part of the early training and education teams for the high school students. The co-op ed coordinators and guidance counselors appear to have been sensitive and intelligent.

The five teens attended schools where the teaching staff willingly adapted (and adopted) teaching methods and schedules to support part-time job assignments by their students.

All five stayed in school and at their jobs. All five didn't move out of the school district during their last two years of high school. All five stayed healthy enough to meet their academic and job responsibilities. Utopia, indeed!

If, as this book is recommending, every high school student should co-op during the 11th and 12th grades, then Anna's large urban high school of 1,800 students would need to place some 900 students in jobs with employers willing to do an enormous amount of attitude and skill training while still running a business.

And the guidance and co-op ed counselors would have to know both the job market and the 900 students well enough to mix and match intelligently and successfully.

The entire academic staff would have to know about job skills and training needs outside the school setting; and every teacher would have to know how to build a curriculum around the needs and abilities of the students, and have to adjust for class attendance on a less-than-consecutive daily basis.

Furthermore, the area's economic stability would have to be such that there were 900 jobs waiting to be filled part-time by students; 900 work supervisors willing to do evaluations of student workers. And all 900 students would have to be alert enough to get to both school and job alternately, for two consecutive years.

As of this writing, less than five percent of high school students across the United States work and go to school in a co-op setting. Less than five percent of the nation's high schoolers have their job supervisors and their academic counselors working together to design learning packages and work out individual evaluation and grading schemes.

Less than five percent of our high school youth (of the more than 90 percent found to hold some kind of job) hold a job which is supported by their regular course work; or conversely, are encouraged to use what they learn at work to complete class assignments.

All the Marys, Hernandezes, Willie Maes, Georges, and Annas, nationwide, need to use the co-op bridge. Building and maintaining this bridge is not too much to ask of schools and businesses.

How much longer will we not construct such bridges for our young people?

Those youngsters who find no bridge flounder; they struggle, stumble, fumble, grope, blunder, shamble, shuffle, totter, and often wallow. Not pretty.

If, as studies apparently confirm, co-op ed can help students make a successful transition from school to work, then it would appear close to criminal -- certainly negligent -- for us not to make this bridge available to every student.

CHAPTER TWO
What is service-learning?

Some academicians are pretty fussy about terminology, and would not agree with my loose definition of cooperative education. For them, work assignments in co-op ed would have to be done in profit-making establishments. They would term a work assignment for a town lawyer (a lawyer on the public payroll) as service-learning.

That is, if a student worked for a law firm in town, and the work was integrated with that student's academic program, then co-op ed would be taking place. But any work in a not-for-profit setting would more likely be called "service-learning."

While giving each of these work/study assignments different names may appear trivial, actually the issue is crucial. That is, the tendency of many service supervisors is not to count the work done by students as "real" work; and the tendency of academicians is to disallow any grains realized while doing community service related to personal values and self-improvement, and hence unrelated to the students' academic coursework.

Many schools have an elective course -- often called "Community Service" -- which they consider to be service-learning. Some educators describe this learning as structured activities that encourage students to reflect on their service experiences, personal values, and the broader social issues related to their service experiences.

I don't agree; I want more than reflection to take place in service-learning.

Whether students work in a private real estate office or in the town tax assessor's office, they should not only expect personal behavior gains and development of adult maturity, but should expect to learn lessons from history about housing and urban development; and from the study of science relevant environmental issues around housing interests; from English classes how to read and understand complex material dealing with housing issues; from the study of mathematics ways to provide the buyer or the town with the best tax situation, etc., etc.

For purposes of this book, most "service-learning" is "co-op ed."

While almost all service-learning is co-op ed, not all co-op ed is service-learning. The very word "service" implies work in the not-for-profit (public) sector. This might mean some independent service to one or more elderly persons in town; or some service rendered to the general public, such as free band concerts on the town green.

It might mean service rendered under the authority of a non-profit agency, such as a United Way member. It might mean work done in conjunction with a service agency (Rotary), or with a service club (Scouts), or within a town agency (fire department).

Service done in a public day-care center fused with academic coursework is service-learning. It follows then that similar work and study done in a private preschool is co-op ed.

Just as I stated in the Introduction that "...all secondary schools should guide and supervise on-the-job training...for all students," so I believe that sometime in each student's school experience his/her on-the-job work assignment should be in a service-learning setting.

To make this happen, teachers would have to adjust coursework readings, research, and writing to supplement the service experience. Easy to see how this takes place for the music department when students learn music which is then performed as part of some civic service. For example, in a nursing home for the elderly; in a hospice; in a homeless shelter; to celebrate a holiday in conjunction with the Meals on Wheels Program, etc.

Equally obvious if the school drama class provides senior citizens with a special production. The service is a culmination of all the study and work done by the students to bring the play to final production.

Not hard to see the connection if students in physical education classes regularly work with youngsters preparing for Special Olympics games, teaching, guiding, and encouraging them in specific sports skills.

Students in art classes, too, are often given the opportunity to sharpen their academic skills while performing an important community service. Perhaps it's a mural for a town-owned space. Maybe it's the offering of mounted drawings for hospice patients. Maybe it's once-a-week lessons in crafts at a senior center. Could be art work done with children in a public day-care center.

Of course, English teachers might well make use of the service part of service-learning for these music, drama, physical education, and art students. Learning how to write advertising copy for the print media is one possible lesson. Learning how to write public information announcements is another. Learning how to describe an emotional experience is another. Learning how to write for radio is another.

The music to be performed might be freshly-written by the students; lyrics if not the actual tune. If the music follows a historic theme, historic research skills may need to be learned. If a literary theme, then literary research skills can be learned.

Those students who offer to work with youth in Special Olympics could fulfill reading assignments to help them better understand how to work with their "pupils."

There is a common tendency for many schools to offer students a single service experience. I know of several schools, for example, which take a day off and for part of just one day everyone does service somewhere.

Sometimes the school decides on a single community-improvement project, and the entire student body may clean up one abused park area. Or perhaps the problem is the need for a homeless shelter, and so in the old-fashioned barn-raising spirit, all hands together complete some type of shelter.

Often, if this is the case, the learning part of this service-learning experience is reduced to such oral or written reports along the genre of: "How I Felt About What I Did." In other words, not much academic integration, but reflection on personal values.

All well and good if the writing done regarding this reflection is writing studied, written, re-written, and re-written as well as edited and commented on by teachers and peers. All well and good if the oral reports given about the service experience strengthen lessons in oral expression, and are refined and refined.

If we take the rehabilitation of an abused public park area, there are many lessons in all social studies classes which could touch on how and why this land has not been better handled. Good research techniques could be honed while finding out why, and who, and when.

Clearly those taking courses in the natural sciences could be given some coursework relevant to the needs in the special park area.

In these instances when service-learning is a single event, often the actual work skills are unskilled labor. Clearing of brush, piling up of trash, carrying, stacking, digging, etc. Hardly meets the conditions generally set for cooperative education. Little skill used, a brief exposure to a work experience, almost no opportunity to improve a skill.

Yet even in such brief encounters, there can be honing of such job-related skills as team work, persistence, consistency, timelines, courtesy toward fellow workers, following orders, and so forth.

If the school authorities treat such one-time service events as a kind of "day off," then, of course, few students will find reason to grow much academically or professionally from the experience. But thoughtful planning from the school authorities, the involvement of all teachers in finding academic significance for the job to be done, should be able to make such an occasion more than "fun," without losing the spirit of fun inherent in such an enterprise.

But the general meaning of co-op ed includes the doing of a job over a sustained period of time, with observable gains in both job skills and related academics.

And this means that service-learning, used as co-op ed, needs to be taken seriously by job supervisors, students, and school personnel. If, for example, co-op ed students are expected to be on the job mornings and in school classrooms afternoons during the school year, then service-learning students should balance their work/study similarly.

A student pondering a possible career as a veterinarian, might spend mornings serving at the humane shelter, and afternoons in classes providing him/her with independent-study assignment around a single research question. History, English, science, all would be used, and not only the humane society supervisors, but a team of teachers would help guide the student through the study process, and be among those grading the results.

That same student might spend the next school year, not in a non-profit organization, but working half days for a private veterinarian clinic; again using a multi-discipline independent-study project to fulfill academic requirements.

It's possible that the school would not be willing to have a student in school only half a day, but require that the work experience one year at the humane society and the following year at the private veterinarian clinic be done by the student late afternoons, weekends, and vacation periods. Some reduction of coursework and homework would be made, but the school would avoid the need to fit a tight course schedule around hundreds of co-op ed work schedules.

Interestingly, many school authorities (actually, that word "many" should be "most") just don't believe students are learning academic skills or improving academic knowledge while they are working at humane societies or at veterinary clinics. Further, they will argue that however well classroom teachers may draw the connections, doing so is not worth the trouble.

For them, the student interested in such a possible career ought to make private service or work arrangements, quite outside the school's jurisdiction.

For them, fusing academic learning and work experience -- learning by doing, -- is not "worth the trouble."

This is often true even of those schools (and whole school districts) which make XXX hours of community service mandatory for graduation.

The Atlanta School System, for example, so often touted as a particularly fine example of mandated student community service, has no service-learning involved. All service work is mandated to be not school-related. Must be done out of school, off school premises, under the supervision of some organization other than the school, and no teacher is expected to provide any coursework or homework assignments which are relevant to the service done.

Other schools, with some form of mandated service activity, even when done on the school premises and/or supervised by school personnel do not fuse the service with the academics.

Fortunately for many of these mandated school programs, the least amount of change would bring co-op ed into play. And by so doing, the service work experience would be exponentially improved.

For example, combining a food-collection drive for the homeless with a study in history of the homeless created by the taking of lands from Native Americans in the economic development from East to West across the United States in the 19th century, would provide students with enormously interesting and provocative reading assignments, and the opportunity to do important research on a topic of life-long concern.

When students in an environmental science class decided to study the Dutch elm disease, and their history and science teachers combined forces, the research in the private and public photo libraries and collections in town helped the students determine where new trees should be planted, and how they should be cared for.

The help the students received from town botanists, historians, garden club members, and librarians -- along with the fun of doing the actual planting of several Dutch elm disease-resistant Liberty Elm trees -- enriched their regular coursework, and added considerably to the material available in their text and modest school library.

The tree planting was, of course, a community service. Continuing care of these seedlings by progressive environmental science classes is a community service. It's also work. And the science learned is reinforced by the planted trees.

It's hard to agree with those school directors and teachers who argue there's no time -- and little purpose -- to service-learning or to co-op ed.

CHAPTER THREE
What is cooperative teacher training?

You'll find two tables at the close of this chapter. They contain some co-op ed statistics which, while not as accurate as one could hope for, are reliable enough to demonstrate that there really are -- at present -- only a very small percent of high school students involved in co-op ed nationwide.

And furthermore, that the number of co-op ed liberal-arts students not enrolled in vocational programs are too few to be significant, hence are not tracked or recorded in any statistical tables assembled by the National Center for Education Statistics.

The problem does not start at the high schools. That is, it's a problem if one thinks students in our high schools should have a co-op ed and/or a service-learning experience. It's a problem if one thinks that learning by doing is not only a viable teaching method, but one which a high percentage of students need in order to achieve any measure of academic success.

No, the problem is in the teacher-training programs in U.S. colleges and universities. That's where the solution is as well.

We'll not have co-op ed an option for every student in every secondary school until all undergraduates studying to be teachers are taught how to fuse or integrate academic subject matter with job performance. And we certainly won't even offer co-op ed to anyone not enrolled in vocational education classes unless students preparing to teach math, science, history, English, language, and the performing arts are taught how to meld student activity with student study.

Is practice teaching co-op ed?

I suppose it is possible for some departments of education to do such a poor job of supervising practice teaching that neither the students involved nor their supervising teachers nor their college instructors make any effort to relate the college coursework to the on-the-job practice-teaching experience.

But I can't imagine there are many such education departments across the nation. What I do expect is that nearly every college has a firm co-op ed-like program in place which integrates reading, research, and study _about_ teaching with on-the-job _actual_ teaching in real classrooms with real pupils. What stops practice teaching from being strict co-op ed at the college level is the fact that student teachers are generally not on a school payroll.

But one reason so few major universities no longer have their teacher trainees do their practice teaching in university-run laboratory schools is the fact that these schools are not the "real world."

That is, they aren't public schools, subject to taxpayers, school boards, unions, etc. And so, during the regular college years, those majoring in education and headed for professional certification, do a co-op ed-like program of on-the-job teaching practice under direct supervision of teachers and administrators.

The best practice-teaching programs use "reflection" to be sure there are personal gains; use observation and commentary by professionals to be sure there are skill gains.

And when the practice teaching is a team effort, using the job-site supervisors both as evaluators and as teachers, working along with the practicing students and the professional college-level faculty, the co-op model is working at top efficiency.

Incredibly, the same university faculty who design these co-op ed like practice-teaching programs in public and private school settings, apparently include no teaching of how to manage co-op ed. Courses in the development of curriculum, for example, do not include lessons in how to fuse academic subject-matter with work experience in the marketplace or the non-profit sector.

Could college departments of education, in calling what future teachers have been doing for nearly 100 years "practice teaching," just possibly have been failing to recognize a form of co-op ed?

Generally special members of the college faculty oversee the practice teaching assignments, not regular academic members of the faculty.

Faculty members do not, by and large, adapt coursework to help their students handle their work assignments. If a student-teacher has difficulty with the teaching of the academics in the work-site classroom, it's generally not the regular education department faculty, or departmental professors in their discipline to whom they go for advice about how to solve this practice-teaching problem.

For example, an English major preparing to be a teacher of high school English, who discovers that he/she might better motivate a classroom full of adolescents if he/she knew how to adapt the composition assignment to prepare a brochure for a popular town event, not only has not been given lessons from pedagogy instructors about how to do this, nor been taught in English composition courses that such adaptation might be necessary for students with limited English-composition ability.

I'll point out an interesting exception to this which will help, I hope, prove the point I'm trying to make. I may not have all the details exact, and beg a literary license, since I know most of this is true.

In the mid 1950s, a cry for help went out from a math ed student at Syracuse University to a member of the math faculty. (Readers: "math ed" refers to a double major in mathematics and education for future math teachers.) The student had been assigned to teach at a junior high, and found his students "hopeless." The math teacher he turned to, Robert B. Davis, is brilliant, earned his Ph.D. in mathematics at a very early age, and had never even been in a public school classroom except as a pupil.

He went to the junior high, listened to part of one class session, went back to the university, designed some exciting and innovative learning activities, and returned to the classroom to do some practice teaching of his own. That was the start of a complete change in this math professor's life. He's still practice teaching, and <u>Plato</u>, the computer program is one of his discoveries. So is what is known as Madison Project Math -- Madison, you'll not be surprised to learn, was the name of the junior high school where he first began thinking of how one might actually teach math concepts using the Socratic method instead of teaching by rote and demand.

Nothing he'd been teaching future teachers about mathematics had been designed to meet the needs so prevalent in that classroom. His conversion, if you will, is the exception and not the rule. Preparation of math teachers coast to coast does not include application of that math to job settings, nor do future math teachers learn how to adapt curriculum to include community service opportunities.

There's considerable evidence that a great many math teachers cannot teach math on their own; instead, they are text-book bound, needing annotations and answer sheets, and only know enough about teaching methods to follow the prescribed script. In other words, their preparation for teaching has been weak both for their academic discipline as well as for their grasp of multiple teaching techniques.

There are some glimmers of light. For example, recreation majors at Green Mountain College provide a nearby public elementary school with a once-a-week after school recreation program consisting of fun games and non-competitive activities. An instructor in the recreation department coordinates the program, and the college students learn from hands-on experience how to apply what they are learning in their academic classes.

But seldom does one hear of such a service-learning experience coordinated for math, history, language arts, or science majors.

I don't know what sort of revolution it will take for colleges and universities to improve the way they prepare future teachers.

Many of us thought that they would change when only the entering freshmen in the lower 50 percent chose to major in education. Somehow we thought that those who headed such departments would be embarrassed to have them filled with the lowest common campus denominators. We were wrong.

Many of us thought that the aftermath of Sputnik would cause dramatic changes in teacher-training methodology and certification requirements. There were, to be fair, a flurry of new programs in the 50s and early 60s. But they did not last, and the pedantic teaching method prevailed. Once again, we were wrong.

The hue and cry over "A Nation At Risk" held out hope that teacher preparation might come in for rigorous scrutiny resulting in better pedagogy, higher standards, and higher quality enrollments. We were wrong.

Instead, the very students who were "at risk" were subjected to the scrutiny, resulting in more tests for them, but not for those who prepared the teachers who held them "at risk." And almost all schemes to improve teacher preparation in consideration today, deal with "outside" programs, not with internal change within schools and departments of education in the 1,000 or so colleges or universities involved in teacher preparation.

I'm enormously active in student community service work, and have been holding workshops, institutes, and courses in that type of cooperative education I call service-learning. The "pupils" are classroom teachers who have never had any instruction in how to adapt the curriculum to integrate work experience and academic skills.

To my knowledge, as of this writing (winter / spring 1990), not one college or university anywhere in the U.S. teaches its potential teachers how to use community service activities to enhance academic coursework and homework. Not one.

You'd think, if not one did, and knowing that these colleges and universities are filled with academicians of the highest qualifications and stature, that I would bow to their superior wisdom. I'd assume there was no reason for education majors to learn how to put into practice John Dewey's philosophy of learning.

There are a few colleges and universities which do teach teachers how to adopt coursework for cooperative education. Almost entirely though, these lessons are reserved for student-teachers majoring in vocational subjects, such as office and health occupations, sales, industrial trades, agriculture, and the like.

I believe I'm correct in stating, though, that at no college which offers cooperative education to undergraduates, do those studying to be teachers ever study of co-op ed. Preparing to be a teacher at Northeastern University in Boston, Massachusetts, the school with the oldest and possibly the largest percentage of co-op ed undergraduates, is, as I understand, entirely separate from the co-op ed programs.

So much so, that entry-level teachers with Northeastern degrees, through the college's efforts, know no more about the "hows" and "whys" of co-op ed than students from the University of Massachusetts in Amherst, which has little or no co-op ed in place.

As the two tables placed at the end of this chapter will show, and even though the statistics are only available through 1982, every indication is that in 1990, fewer than five percent of all secondary students are involved in co-op ed.

Looking at that figure, deans of education might conclude that co-op ed was a matter of little interest and perhaps even less importance. And they would be right, if the following were true:

- That the best and brightest undergraduates were signing up to major in education.

- That graduates of their schools were not the teachers involved in the failure of half the nation's school children.

- That learning by doing was an inadequate and inappropriate teaching method.

- That the secondary school years were not the time when adolescents should learn primary job skills and appropriate work-place behavior.

- That the doing of civic service would not enhance the teaching of civics.

HIGH SCHOOL CO-OP ENROLLMENT
BY OCCUPATION

1980 * 1981 * 1982

PROGRAM	1980	1981	1982
Marketing/Distributive	198,636	193,215	206,315
Trabe & Industrial	151,002	150,298	135,292
Business	120,501	146,319	191,743
Home Economics	39,216	44,522	47,441
Other	33,028	30,460	17,439
Agriculture	25,342	28,732	72,006 *
Health Occupations	19,842	20,007	20,950
Technical	9,997	10,548	38,852 **
Totals	597,564	623,741	730,038

Source: National Center for Education Statistics, ED

* Rise is not in farm work, per se, but in agri-business and related nursery/florist/gardening occupations.

** Reflects impact of computer industry.

HIGH SCHOOL CO-OP ED ENROLLMENT
IN 1980
COMPARED TO ALL VOC ED
ENROLLMENTS

Program	All Students	Co-Op Ed Students
Office Occupations	1,970,518	120,176
Trade & Industry	1,792,052	149,373
Distributive Ed	601,275	198,380
Health Occupations	455,129	19,996
Agriculture	384,940	25,332
Technical	387,117	10,282
Home Economics	242,087	39,096
Other	146,390	33,028
Totals	* 5,979,508	**595,663

Source: National Center for Education Statistics, ED

---

*   Table 5 gives 11,763,539 as total vocational student enrollment for 1980. Perhaps the radical difference comes from the counting method, and the lower figure here represents only those high school students enrolled in programs also served by co-op ed.

**   This figure is 1,901 students fewer than the enrollment figure given in Table 1. Most important, though, is whether, in 1980, co-op enrollment was 5% of the total vocational enrollment, or 10% as indicated on this chart.

42

CHAPTER FOUR

Some assumptions and what follows.

(1)   It is better for a high school student to have some work experience than to have none at all.

(2)   It is better for a student to learn good work habits such as promptness, courtesy, follow-through, orderliness, honesty, and so forth than not to have such an opportunity.

(3)   It is better for a student to learn at least one measurable rudimentary job skill than to leave school with only academic credits.

(4)   It is better for a student to have guided work experience than to hold random, minimally-supervised jobs.

(5)   It is better for a student to receive school- supervised work experience and skill training in a real job setting than in a school shop or simulated workplace.

Before you find yourself agreeing with the first assumption -- certainly sounds reasonable -- let's take a look at what's offered most students in most U.S. public secondary schools.

There's the college-prep track or program or course offerings -- or however it is categorized in your community. In only the rarest of instances is any thought whatever given in any U.S. public school to including credit for work experience for students taking college-prep and advanced placement courses.

And since school credit is the "coin" of the high school realm, and particularly in the college-prep program, the message given by schools to students is that "no work experience" is necessary.

That message also includes the implication that schools have "done their duty" by their college-bound students even though they have not included work experience as part and parcel of that school diet.

In addition to the college-bound, most high schools place a strong percentage of their students in a "general education" program which, like the college-prep curriculum, does not include skill training or work experience. Instead, these students are offered a selection of courses, athletic opportunities, and club activities all providing credits toward a graduation degree or certificate, but no school-sponsored or school-credited work experience.

What's left, nationwide, is a small percentage of high school students who, with school assistance, get sound work experience. And yet, what's also true is that a huge percentage (some put it at as much as 90%) of all students work during their high school years.

One argument often given why schools don't include more students in co-op ed programs is that employers are unwilling to do the necessary training of unskilled youth workers, and therefore co-op ed programs cannot expand.

The contention obviously flies in the face of reality; thousands of employers want and seek student workers, and provide necessary training, equipment, uniforms, job benefits, etc.

Another argument put forward is the one connected to course load and time. Hard working college-prep students, with their heavy academic schedule of courses and homework, and extra-curricular activities, so goes the argument, have no time or energy left to co-op. Or a comparable argument: College-prep students cannot afford to "sandwich" course work between work assignments, and need to concentrate on their academics so that they can get into the college of their choice.

These arguments, though, don't hold up against the results of nearly 80 years of secondary school level co-op ed programs carried out by college-bound students. In fact, for many of the highly-selective college admission's officers, a transcript showing a co-op ed work experience is more often a "plus" and provides the college another measure of why one student seems to be more promising than another.

Moving along to the second assumption, good work habits, here we have a clear message from employers in all sectors of the economy. Even more than job skills --personnel officers nationwide contend -- entry-level workers, particularly teen-age high school graduates, need to bring good work habits to the job site.

"We'll gladly train them in the necessary skills," they argue, "but send them to us already knowing what it is to follow orders, pay attention, be part of a working team, call in when they can't get to work..."

The call for an understanding of "teamwork" is particularly appropriate for today's school officials and teachers. It is habitual today for teachers to require that an enormous amount of academic school work be done without teamwork -- in virtual isolation of students from students. Yet most jobs call for a blending of ideas, skills, talents, and elbow grease by teams of workers.

Many of the same good work habits are good study habits; they can be taught and honed by academic teachers. Asking that a group of students work to find a solution to a science or mathematics problem isn't teaching students to cheat, it's teaching them how adults attack -- and solve -- problems.

Which brings us to assumption #3, and its call for students to leave school with a job skill as well as with sufficient academic credits. In general, U. S. public schools have not accepted this assumption as a guiding principle for syllabus and curriculum. And when they have offered skill training, it has more often than not been limited to a school setting, and not worked out in conjunction with a non-school employer.

Sewing, cooking, typing, radio repair, small engine repair, electrical wiring, welding, brick laying, even word-processing skills have, in traditional vocational or technical education classes been learned in a classroom setting or school shop, with next to no time spent practicing the skill,--while under school supervision,--in a real work site.

That is, schools don't provide real jobs except in cooperative education programs; or where the school work site is to all intents and purposes an "outside" work site. For example, when the school operates a working motel serving the public and uses co-op students in all facets of management, maintenance, and service.

And this brings us to the assumption that students will learn more and be more attractive to future employers if the work they do while still students is guided by both the school personnel and work supervisors.

If we look back at Mary's school/work experience, we can see how her interest in sports, and her school's interest in her retailing future combined to place her on an appropriate career path with good work habits, and sound retail sales skills. Further, there was no diminution of her varsity sports activity or her academic coursework.

Bookkeeping, accounting, public speaking, contemporary American thought: These courses, and others, aided Mary academically while her job supervisors helped her deal intelligently with customers, with sound business practices, with an understanding of how to use her "outside" interests to improve her job performance.

For Willie Mae and Hernandez, data processing in a classroom setting might have seemed "routine" or "abstract," but when your employer, a bank, counts on your data for making business transactions, that's serious and tangible.

While Willie Mae or Hernandez might have picked up some good and important work habits had they mowed lawns, baby-sat, washed and bussed dishes, served fast food, and worked a toy counter as a sales clerk, neither would have honed such a skill as data processing.

Entry-level, dead-end jobs can teach an active teenager a lot of lessons, but not as many as they can learn by developing a skill, and by integrating their academics with their work experience.

George was fortunate to have a science teacher who was quick to recognize what it would do both for George and for his college-bound chemistry students to work together experimenting and writing up material on cleansing agents.

And Anna, who wanted to play word games, lead skits, put on puppet shows, and help develop toddlers' language skills sorely needed to learn about childrens' literature from a scholar. Anna needed not only to learn to want to work, but needed to see a reason to study so that her work experience would be fulfilling.

She needed the public speaking lessons, so that she would know how to help her little ones with diction and pronunciation. And from her ecology lessons at school, Anna could devise activities for her charges which would sharpen their love for and understanding of the natural world.

At first, it must have been very difficult for Anna's supervisor in the day-care center to get Anna past the stage of being a passive babysitter, and to become engaged with wholesome learning activities for the children. But how important that Anna got that chance. And that she got it in a work setting where failure to measure up would mean being fired.

Of course, if Anna's school had run a day-care center along professional lines, serving the public, and enforcing rules and regulations, then Anna could have gotten a similar work/study experience under the one school roof.

But, I would argue, if Anna's class had just invited a few children in for a few days a semester, that would not have provided Anna with the full work experience; with the full professional standards necessary in a real job setting. Yes, Anna might have developed some skills in dealing with toddlers if she had only gotten jobs as a baby sitter, but not to the same degree, nor with the expert evaluation and assistance which come from working with strong professionals.

CHAPTER FIVE

What is the role of business and co-op ed?

The Committee for Economic Development (CED) has come out strongly in favor of cooperative education. Their major report on schools and businesses, printed and distributed in 1988, states:

> "We recommend that schools work with local businesses to design and implement better work-study and/or cooperative education programs, and that state and local governments assign these programs a high priority in policy and financing decisions.

> "...high school vocational education programs that do not teach specific job skills have not been successful either in terms of providing good remedial education or adequate employability skills and do not provide necessary compensatory education.

> "Many low-achieving students and dropouts never learn the basic skills and work-related behaviors that are necessary for success on the job. As a consequence, these youths have fewer opportunities for employment, and even if employed, they are less productive and adaptable.

"We urge schools to improve the school-to-work transition [the bridge] by making greater use of programs that provide outside work experience related to classroom learning.

"We encourage a careful expansion of cooperative education and similar programs, particularly in schools where they do not now exist, combined with a more thorough analysis of the program's outcome. We also recommend that business participate in such efforts."

While the CED "recommends that business participate...", I contend we're past the "recommendation" stage. And that without the participation of both private businesses and non-profit organizations, we'll not have an expansion of co-op ed.

Teacher training at the university level is not going to change unless business interests force it to do so. Student teachers will not be able to take courses which teach curriculum development which accommodate a fusion of academics and job skills unless major tax-paying businesses demand that a large percent of our future teachers be trained in how to support and manage co-op ed.

Universities won't train teachers for jobs which do not exist; and co-op ed is not available throughout our public schools nationwide. In addition, school administrators are not going to change their programs to include co-op ed, unless they are forced to do so from "outside." That is, they would change if teacher-training changed.

Research studies done by business and industry have consistently shown that there is a positive correlation between employment rates for young adults and students who work during the final two years of high school.

But every survey of school principals and guidance counselors finds these educationists unwilling to believe this research. They overwhelmingly argue that students who hold down jobs in addition to attending school, don't do as well as students who do not mix work and study.

"Don't do as well" at what? Youngsters who do not learn any job skills or positive job attitudes before completing grade 12, or leaving school at age 16, are entering young adulthood at a distinct disadvantage. We know what happens to these young people; overwhelmingly they make up the under-employed and the unemployed.

What makes these school officials believe in the fiction that job skills are neither important for young adults to learn or that it's none of the school's business to prepare secondary-level students for employability?

I'm going to argue that both the business community and the universities have had a hand in maintaining this fiction. The universities by not including co-op ed and service-learning instruction for all teacher candidates. And the businesses by spending their own funds, time, and energy to train entry-level employees in what they could (and should) have learned both in classrooms and in work-study assignments.

Certainly schools will not offer service-learning and co-op ed experiences to more than a fraction of enrolled students unless both the business and independent sectors agree to provide training experiences for high school students in conjunction with their academic teachers.

Furthermore, schools will not spend any of their annual funds to evaluate these programs unless businesses not only help in the evaluation designs, but in their costs. While businesses regularly put aside funds for research, this is not true of schools or school districts.

And because school administrators have not been in the evaluation and analysis business regarding the value of specific school programs, they need all the help they can get from the business sector to do the sort of analysis demanded by cooperative education.

Often school administrators, defending their failure to provide co-op ed, give as an excuse that the right kinds of jobs are not to be found, and hence to adapt curriculum for so many different job requirements would be fiscally prohibitive and an administrative nightmare.

Not true. In the 1970s, women were employed in the following occupations ranked in order of numbers of employees:

> Secretarial
> Sales
> Bookkeeping
> Elementary school teaching
> Waitressing
> Typing
> Sewing
> Nursing
> Maids in private households

And men were employed as:

> Managers/administrators
> Sales workers
> Foremen
> Truck drivers
> Farmers
> Janitors
> Carpenters
> Automobile mechanics
> Machine operators

The U. S. Bureau of Labor Statistics estimates that the "fastest growing occupations for both males and females up through 1995" will be:

> Building custodians
> Cashiers
> Secretaries
> General office clerks
> Sales clerks

There is no school community too rural, nor too urban, unable to provide co-op ed assignments in these five occupations.

The fastest growth through at least 1995, based on percentage increase of newly-created jobs, calls for:

> Computer service technicians
> Legal assistants
> Computer systems analysts
> Computer programmers
> Computer operators

Note, these are all service occupations. And all, even the legal assistantships, require the use of advanced technological equipment.

I think we may be at an important crossroads for co-op ed because of these occupational changes. It becomes increasingly indefensible for a high school (or even a vocational center) to try to "create" the same technical setting in a school shop or classroom as is found in an actual place of business.

What makes eminent sense is for students to co-op in businesses, government offices, and non-profit organizations where they can gradually learn enough to become at the very least computer operators. Each business, even each office or work station at a job site, may have a different computer set up, and require special computer skill knowledge.

This means the job of the school is to teach not only the theory of computer science, but about the various uses, so that the student who co-ops with one type of word processing equipment, for example, will know about others while developing a single specific job-related skill.

Employers, looking for entry-level 16-18 year old employees, are quite prepared to teach each new employee the use of their special computer equipment, but if a business has two candidates for the same job, and one has had a co-op placement with computer experience, and the other has not held any school-related job assignments but has taken high school computer classes, the co-op ed student has the edge.

And what little follow-up evidence is available indicates that high school co-op ed students tend to be employed five years after graduation at a significantly higher rate of pay than regular vocational education graduates, and at a much higher rate than school dropouts or those with a general high school diploma.

This being the case, and as a later savings in training and re-training costs for all employers, it would seem not only fiscally prudent but humanitarian as well for all businesses (public and private) to encourage all secondary schools to offer co-op ed for every student.

Paul Barton, writing for the Grant Commission's "Youth and America's Future," after quoting Rupert Evans and Edwin Herr that "studies of the economics of cooperative education have shown higher rates of return on investment than in other types of programs," cites six advantages of co-op ed.

- Learning occupational skills is aided by real experience.
- The school and employer must work together, identifying weaknesses and remedying them before graduation.
- Joint work-study programs provide a job connection [bridge] after graduation.
- The market test is applied all the time; employers will not participate in imparting skills for which there is no demand.
- Cooperative style education reduces the problem of keeping up-to-date equipment in classrooms or shops.

■ In general, such arrangements force schools and employers to talk with each other.

Here's a conversation which school authorities and business managers should have held long ago. Comes from studies done by the Center for Public Resources. Seems that the same questions were put to a group of school personnel and business officials.

Question: Are school students, in general, receiving "adequate" job skills preparation?

Answer: Some three-fourths of the school people said "Yes." More than half the business people said "No."

Question: In which academic skills are school graduates most deficient?

Answer: The school people answered "reading" the business people, "speaking, listening, mathematics, and science."

Question: How important is scientific knowledge in all job categories including low-skilled ones?

Answer: The school people said, "Not very;" the business people said, "Very."

Changing the school curriculum and the structure of classes, moving from competitive to cooperative student groupings, foregoing didactic teaching and norm-referenced tests for the Socratic method and portfolios expressing accomplishments, opening up a partnership relationship with the business community culminating in co-op ed assignments, and developing continuing involvement in community service and service-learning aren't ideas to be mulled over by dreamers.

They are imperatives.

I think we've tested long enough whether those running our public schools and training our future teachers want to make these changes so badly that they are willing -- on their own -- to take the required risks, and to do whatever extra is necessary for the changeover.

Business, industry, service organizations, government offices: You hold the key to school betterment. You hold the key to an improved national work force.

In almost every school district nationwide, you employers are the majority taxpayers -- your tax monies go directly to maintenance and operation of your local public schools. You are in a key position to demand needed change.

We're going to need:

- Hundreds of thousands of building custodians skilled in the operation of enormously expensive and complex equipment.

- Hundreds of thousands of cashiers who are able to remain accurate at the use of inventorying machines, while providing service to an impatient public.

- Hundreds of thousands of secretaries skilled in word-processing, and able to maintain flows of material from a plethora of sources.

- Hundreds of thousands of general office and sales clerks with instant recall of multiple items, an understanding of computer technology, and a love of detail.

■ Hundreds upon hundreds of thousands of adults who know how to service all types of computer and communications equipment.

Where are those several million employees going to come from? They are already here; they are in grades one through twelve.

If each business were to double the number of co-op ed students it regularly accommodates, we would go from about one million co-ops to two million. But let's jump higher.

Let's have every non-profit organization and every business now without a co-op ed student take on just one; well, maybe just two!

And let's concentrate on high school students who don't expect to go directly on to a post-secondary institution. Let those who do go on, co-op at the undergraduate level. But just for the next decade, let's see what would happen if every business and every non-profit organization helped each local school work out a co-op like educational plan for one or two potential drop outs or terminating high schoolers each year.

We know that there would be a dramatic change in numbers. We can assume that with as many as 30 percent of all secondary students expecting high school faculty to integrate academic coursework with job-related skills to support their co-op ed assignments, that the teacher-training institutions would have to prepare their graduates for this curriculum design process.

And we can easily assume the following, if and when the business community involves all local public high schools in high-quality co-op ed programs.

- More students will stay in school through the 12th grade.

- More courses will be team-taught by school faculty and people on loan from the business community.

- Service-learning will swell the volunteer ranks of all human services organizations in all communities nationwide.

- Teacher-training institutions will record an upgrade in the quality of those majoring in education with an eye to becoming public school teachers.

- The non-public preparatory secondary schools will begin offering co-op ed and service-learning programs for all students.

- More states will pass more laws permitting part-time teaching by non-certificated college graduates in public secondary schools.

- Fewer norm-referenced tests will be given or used as determinants for student next steps.

- Co-op ed at the college level will double or triple in numbers, and come under severe academic scrutiny.

CHAPTER SIX
What is the co-op bridge?

The CED (Committee for Economic Development) defined the cooperative education bridge most succinctly as: "school-to-work transition."

Webster's Second Collegiate Dictionary defines "bridge" in part as: "a thing that provides connection, contact, or transition."

And Roget's Thesaurus gives the following synonyms for the noun "bridge:" "connection, connector, tie, link, coupling, bond, band, nexus, joint.

Co-op ed is that essential link between full-time schooling and full-time employment.

Talking about work. Watching people work. Reading about economics and business. Visiting a work site. Observing the performance of specific job skills. These are among the many approach-the-bridge essentials. But they are not the connector or bond.

Doing odd jobs or unskilled labor outside of school. Lab work. Classroom experiments. Shop classes. One-time volunteer activities in the community. These are approach-the-bridge enhancements. They make possible the transition; they are not the bridge itself.

The following analogy may help. Nearly every 15-year old wants to get across a very important bridge at age 16, or soon thereafter -- the transition from car passenger to car driver! Talking about driving. Watching people drive. Reading about cars and driving. Visiting a car lot. Washing, cleaning, polishing, even repairing cars.

These are important, but they are not the bridge, that on-the-road practice which is absolutely essential before a car passenger becomes a responsible car driver.

I grew up on a farm, and drove farm machinery starting at the age of 11; hence the mechanics of driving were well known to me long before I was old enough to take my driving test. But I did not gain either the skill or confidence to be a road driver until I had spent countless hours guided by an adult practicing both on country roads and in city traffic, and in all types of weather conditions including ice, snow, and mud.

Of course, one reason I've chosen car driving to help illustrate my point about the need for a co-op ed bridge, is the fact that so many secondary schools do provide the driver-ed bridge, while they fail to provide the job-skill bridge. I agree, driver-ed is important, particularly for youngsters who live in homes without an adult driver who could provide this bridge. But I'd also argue that schools have their priorities backwards. The bridge or transition from school to work is much more the business of educators than is the teaching of road-driving skills, and providing of car-driving time. If a school hasn't the resources and time for both, co-op ed and driver ed, let the schools integrate on-the-job experience with sound academics, and let the private sector provide the driver training.

Let me move to another analogy. As early as fifty years ago, nearly every school teacher and administrator was the first person in a family to have graduated from a four-year college. Since each secondary school wanted to place all the top students in a post-secondary institution, some bridge was needed to help with this transition, particularly since nearly three-fourths of all school-aged children in the 1940s and '50s lived in homes with no college graduates.

Therefore the college counseling program was initiated. Colleges wanted schools to have counselors as it gave them a single contact point and made their jobs easier. Teacher training departments at colleges and universities recognized the importance and growth potential of this school job, and instituted programs to teach this bridging skill at both the undergraduate and graduate levels.

What was done to accommodate the creation of a bridge between high school and college certainly can be done for the school-to-work transition. Businesses should find co-op ed counselors, and co-op ed programs similarly useful. And once the business community begins communicating with co-op ed departments, schools would, as they did with driver-ed and college guidance, adapt the school syllabus to include on-the-job work experience. And the tardy colleges and universities, just as they now proudly offer courses related to college counseling, would begin offering courses related to cooperative education.

Which comes first, the chicken or the egg? Which comes first, co-op ed in schools or pre-service teacher-training in co-op ed? Which comes first, a demand for co-op ed jobs from the schools or from local businesses?

It's my contention that schools and colleges have proved their lack of interest in co-op ed for so long that it will take the business community to be the "egg" which hatches the co-op ed chicken. Also my contention that the cost to businesses of providing basic academic and job skills for entry-level employees will become prohibitive; and that having high school students begin to make the all-important connection between sound work behavior and adequate job performance will spur businesses to insist that all secondary schools make co-op ed available to all students headed for and hoping for full-time employment.

The College for Human Services in New York City, designed and directed by Audrey Cohen, is a "co-op ed bridge" in its entirety. Ms. Cohen has turned the regular college curriculum on its ear. Every single student does co-op ed. And every single academic class is interdisciplinary. No one teaches history, or math, or science, or language arts as separate disciplines to students at the college for Human Services as is done in nearly every other college in the nation.

Instead, all academic disciplines are fused to provide lessons supporting such issues as management, structure, personnel, service, etc. It's an exciting and dramatic way to integrate on-the-job experiences with important lessons in academics. At the present time, an effort is under way -- directed by Audrey Cohen and some of the College for Human

Services staff -- to introduce a similar program at the junior and senior high school level in both New York City and Florida.

In the case of the College for Human Services, my definition of "bridge" is exemplified in their entire program; that's certainly one way to make co-op ed central to each student's schooling.

By integrating academics with job skills; that is, by fusing classroom learning with on-the-job demands, students learn not only what it is to work, but how to work, and further, how to use "book learning" to advance on a job site.

The co-op ed student holding down an afternoon job 20 hours a week as a clerk in a retail store or business office needs to be taught some accounting, some business theory, speaking and listening skills, business arithmetic, and other clerking skills.

Yet history courses are equally important for the clerk, providing the beginnings of an understanding of how our U.S. political and economic system works. Sound teaching in math classes, beyond applied arithmetic and bookkeeping skills, should provide the co-op ed clerk with an understanding of logic, organization, and structure -- three essential abilities for anyone planning a career in retailing.

From course work in the arts, the student should develop a sense of beauty, culture, and grace -- again, essential learnings for one whose task it is to meet and serve the public. Language study, in addition to the lessons taught about the power of thinking, provide essential experiences in good communication.

Rather than considering co-op ed time as time away from academics, academicians and subject-matter specialists should understand that this is "laboratory time" for the exploration of the fresh ideas coming from literature, the arts, the sciences, and social studies.

Is co-op ed something new in public schooling? Was there ever a bridge or link between school and work?

No to the first question; yes to the second.

Of course, the business of linking academic lessons with work experience is as old as time. But in U.S. education history, a professor of engineering (Herman Schneider) at the University of Cincinnati is credited with the first formal work-study program in 1906. Prof. Schneider stated then that the purpose of cooperative education was "not only to help students get jobs, but to monitor their performance to assure a correlation with academic course work."

Three years later in 1909, Northeastern University in Boston began using a co-op ed program similar to that at the University of Cincinnati. And eight years later in 1914, the president of the National Cash Register Corporation in Dayton, Ohio, worked out a co-op ed program with the local board of education at the high school level.

By 1922, co-op ed moved from technical fields to the liberal arts beginning with a program at Antioch College in Antioch, Ohio, and in 1932, Bennington College in Bennington, Vermont, required -- as it does today -- an 8-week field work term integrated for each student with his/her academic program in the liberal arts. A student studying poetry, for example, might intern at the headquarters of a poetry journal; a voice major work with an organization sponsoring a chorus; a student of drama might take a job with a theater company; and so forth.

Since each student is expected to carry out field work each year, any student not sure whether literature or theater is more interesting as a full-time career, may explore both careers on the job, in a studio, and in the classroom. Hard statistics about how many co-op students go to work for one of their business sites are not available, but those long involved in making these arrangements think that fifty percent is a fair estimate.

Research among co-op employers, indicates about the same percentage of full-time hirings after part-time exploration. Yet job supervisors repeatedly make the point that they do not enter into cooperative education to bring specific students over the bridge to lure them into becoming future employees, but to provide the bridge for any student, knowing that they will benefit because of the linkage. But those are the reactions of employers who may themselves have been co-op students while in college and now welcome high school and college co-ops in the businesses.

Dr. Morgan V. Lewis is a scientist with the National Center for Research in Vocational Education located at Ohio State University in Columbus. It is his contention that a fundamental constraint on the expansion of cooperative education is the lack of willingness of employers to assume an expanded role in skill training.

"There are considerations arising from the nature of our economic system," Dr. Lewis wrote in a paper for the Grant Commission on Work, Family and Citizenship, "that lead me to be skeptical about the possibility of a major expansion of cooperative education. A basic tenet of our economy is that the operation of free markets is the most effective way to set priorities and allocate resources. The primary role of public policy governing the economy is to encourage free markets and to ease the hardships that their operations sometimes cause.

"This policy extends to labor markets where national policy has generally encouraged occupational and geographic mobility of workers. This policy has enabled the economy to change rapidly and has avoided the problems of shortages in critical skill areas. If shortages develop, jobs are modified and workers with related skills are reassigned. The policy does, however, reduce the incentive for employers to offer training in occupations that require extensive preparation before a worker becomes productive. With high rates of job change, employers may not realize a return on the costs of such training. Extended training is a risky investment which relatively few employers are willing to make.

"It is these characteristics of the labor market that, in my judgment, explain the willingness of society to provide the wide array of opportunities for institutionally-based vocational-technical training available in this country. The training that public institutions provide offers the individuals who obtain jobs that use their training an advantage in the competition for the preferred jobs in our society. Employers who hire trained workers benefit from their increased productivity. The private and social losses incurred by individuals who do not obtain jobs related to their training are borne directly by these individuals and only indirectly by employers and the public, in general, through the taxes they pay.

"These characteristics also have made it difficult to expand cooperative education." Citing a study regarding the provision of part-time jobs for disadvantaged young people, Dr. Lewis maintained that even with a 100% wage subsidy, employers were reluctant to hire disadvantaged youths. With a 100% subsidy, only 18% of potential employers were willing to participate; a 75% subsidy reduced that to 1 out of 10 possible employers. Dr. Lewis commented:

"These figures reflect minimum levels of the willingness of employers to offer part-time jobs, because young people from disadvantaged backgrounds are not viewed favorably by many employers." He concluded: "These findings do not lead to much optimism that cooperative programs would be able to serve large numbers of those young people who have the most difficulty succeeding in school and making the transition from education to employment."

Curiously, I would cite identical policies and employer concerns as the very reason to expand cooperative education. Employee training costs money, as well as lost productivity time during the training period. And naturally employers want to provide extensive training only for those employees with whom they wish to have a long-term relationship. Therefore, co-op employers, who need only provide minimal training at miminal cost for their unpaid or least-paid student-workers, have a ready-made employee pool.

For the co-op ed student, while the pay is minimal at best, and the training generally only at the entry level, the job experience is invaluable, and, like the employer, gives the student a view from the inside about that organization in particular, and the job field in general.

In other words, the preferred bridge for the student is the preferred bridge for the employer, both have every reason to use it.

- Students don't really have a choice -- only way they can get on-the-job experience is on a job.

- Employers don't really have a choice -- only way they can hire new employees with some prior job experience is to provide job experience.

CHAPTER SEVEN
What happens when there is no bridge?

It's pretty tough going for those students for whom there is no bridge from K-12 schooling to either a job or higher education. And even more difficult when our schools do not provide the necessary approach roadways. But today, we find thousands of our young people stranded on the way to a bridge.

Come with me to grade four. Almost all fourth grade teachers, assign homework in basic skill subjects. A typical assignment might come from a set of spelling words introduced one day, and tested for accuracy one or two days later, with practice time supposed to have taken place at home. Or, the homework might consist of a set of arithmetic examples in column addition, following lessons in how to carry out this function given by the teacher during class time.

In these instances, the homework assigned by the 4th grade teachers needs a teacher. Obviously the schoolteachers expect the home teacher to bring the pupil from not knowing to knowing; from not using to regular use; from not understanding to comprehension. This supervised practice is supposed to improve accuracy, precision, speed, wisdom, etc.

Now, let's picture a fourth grader getting off a bus or walking each school-day afternoon to a two-room apartment which houses a single parent, several younger siblings, an occasional adult visitor, but no one with a college or even a high school degree. There's no separate room for the student to use to get away from the younger children or from the sound of the television which is on day and night, and no study materials such as a dictionary or math manipulatives.

Let's imagine another fourth grader who lives in a trailer with a single parent, and older as well as younger siblings. The fourth grader's grandmother is on welfare, as is his mother. The trailer is on an old wood lot at the back of his grandmother's property. None of the fourth graders' relatives liked either spelling or arithmetic when at school; none have attended college; only a few attended high school for any length of time. But this fourth grader's mother wants him to finish school, and she tells him no supper until the homework is done. He does it in fits and starts with no supervision.

Of course, elementary school teachers should never give such assignments to those pupils who have no adequate support at home. And, of course, 4th graders (as well as 5th, 6th, 7th...), whose home life provides work space, appropriate materials, adult supervision by high school graduates, and enthusiasm for such academic skill activity, will return to school prepared for the next spelling words and progressive steps in arithmetic.

That is, those pupils will have had the kind of support needed; the others, without that help, will fall farther and farther behind.

I didn't pick 4th grade at random. This is the grade level when most teachers begin giving the kind of homework assignments designed to improve basic skills. Unfortunately, most teachers ignore the wide range of learning abilities and home help situations of their class of 25, 30, 35, or 40 students, and generally give the exact homework assignment to all their pupils.

And not surprisingly, those very same teachers discover that the children who do their homework under the direction of the most skillful home help, do best in class work and class tests. Correspondingly, those children who fail at this type of homework, generally fail in class, progressively falling behind.

Clearly the children who begin failing academically starting at the fourth grade level, are not those students who are -- during the high school years -- provided with the bridge to college, either in course selection or in guidance counseling.

Then it is reasonable to ask: Will the high-schoolers without access to a bridge to college be provided, instead, with a bridge to a full-time job? Unfortunately, the answer generally is "No."

By and large today, those few students allowed to co-op, at most five percent of all secondary school students, must be doing well academically. And so those missing the academic approach runway appear doomed to miss both the bridge to college, and the bridge from school to work.

Interestingly enough, the few experiments I know about which have given co-op ed assignments to academically marginal students have been surprisingly effective. The students discover while on a job how important basic learning skills are to job satisfaction, and this has resulted in their doing whatever they needed in order to cross that all-important academic bridge; and from there to cross the bridge to full-time employment.

Public/Private Ventures (P/PV) has been experimenting with dropout-prone high schoolers in a program they name BRIDGE. They are seeing considerable progress. The following is a brief description of their experiment: "In addition to regular classes, participants attend a special BRIDGE class at least five periods a week for three semesters, and get academic credit for attending.

"BRIDGE students enter the program in the middle of the 9th grade...having to score at least two grades behind their peers in reading and math. The BRIDGE class offers instruction in job-related skills, life skills and study skills, and connects all of this with the academic skills taught in other classes.

"BRIDGE youth are also offered help with personal and family problems by BRIDGE staff and community volunteers, a combination of work and education during two summers, and a place in their school's existing school-to-work transition program in the 11th grade." What they are having to do is to provide not only "catch-up" lessons, but ongoing support which, for whatever set of reasons, is missing.

While I was a senior program officer with the National Institute of Education (NIE) in the 1970s, I introduced an experiment in five poor rural school districts to test whether giving a co-op ed experience to a potential dropout might result in the student staying in school, and getting a job directly after completing grade 12.

We arranged for 20 fifteen-year olds in each of the participating schools whom the academic teachers said were "poor" academically, to leave school full time for one marking period, and to hold down unskilled jobs at local work sites. The students were paid the minimum hourly wage through a grant from the NIE, and given special counseling to help with job interviews, job skills, and positive work attitudes.

Nineteen of the 20 at each site (95 of the full 100) returned to school after completing their work assignments determined to finish, and guaranteed employment at their work site if -- and only if -- they completed grade 12. At each high school, it was one of the young women involved who did not return; instead, in all five cases unwed motherhood intervened. But the other 95 young men and women did so well in their jobs that their supervisors promised them jobs after graduation. And all 95 went on to complete school, many returning to their same co-op employers.

That's the good news.

The bad news? None of those school districts continued the experiment using their own funds. (And I know of very few school districts which offer this alternative to their "at risk" teenagers.) Why? Why didn't those five schools in Iowa, Montana, Delaware, Alabama, and North Dakota, who saw how successful such an alternative program could be, continue it, expand it, and make it a regular part of their high school program?

Even though I may be labeled a "radical," I think one reason this program is not in place nationwide, is the fact that schools would rather invest funds in the college-bound than the vocation-bound. Comprehensive high schools, nationwide, pride themselves not on the number of students who graduate into full-time, entry-level employment, but on the number accepted at the college of their choice.

In addition, those whose task it is to measure school quality more often than not cite average test scores in academic aptitude and achievement, and do not take into consideration a school's ability to place co-op ed students in the job of their choice.

Because norm-referenced tests like the SAT, have grown so in importance and are often the key ingredient in the measurement of school "success," many schools do not have marginal students take the exams, hence creating a false "average" which is no average. In the case of the SAT, for example, often fewer than 20 percent of the eligible students statewide actually take the examinations, skewing the statistics, and continuing the myth that high schools have but one goal -- preparation for the next academic grade level. And further, that schools should be judged on their test "average," regardless of how many students don't even take the tests.

I believe if it were not for the interest expressed in dropout rates by parents, the business community, and the feeling-burdened property-tax payers, we'd probably never talk about "at risk" students, nor admit what a travesty high school is for all those students who need and want to make the transition from school to work, and who are given no instruction in how to cross this bridge.

School authorities are concerned about their failures, yet the general impression they want the public at large to believe is that dropouts cause themselves! Few school administrators or teachers want to believe that their 4th grade homework assignments are the beginning of the end for half of their pupils.

While I have nothing but the deepest sympathy and admiration for all who serve in our public school system, and recognize they must deal with the most severely disadvantaged of the nation's children, I take umbrage at their treatment of these "at risk" pupils.

Of all children, those struggling academically need in every way possible to have their mental arithmetic and applied quantitative reasoning so integrated that concepts and applications fuse together in meaningful and productive ways. Not only within classrooms should all school youngsters be given practice activities which exemplify "learning by doing," but homework assignments should be individualized and used to strengthen each pupil in each pupil's needs, within each pupil's home context.

Combining community service activities with classroom lessons starting right at kindergarten would help in the building of that all-important bridge to success.

Here let me give a series of possible service-learning activities culminating in a full year of co-op ed in grade 12, designed to meet the needs of all pupils, not just those with learning problems and/or a disadvantaged home situation. These activities aren't pie in someone's sky, they are real, and maybe it's in your school system that they are happening.

Kindergarten

■ The children, daily, fold and decorate napkins to be used by residents in one or more nursing homes. Arithmetic lessons can be based on the necessary counting. Art, penmanship, drawing, and language arts lessons can be based on the decorating.

■ The children are in charge of cleaning the table tops in the school's cafeteria, using this daily task for arithmetic practice and health lessons.

Grade One

■ Each pupil has a "pen pal" in a hospital, nursing home, or a senior citizen living alone. The children regularly send letters, stories, and drawings to their correspondents. The pen pal activities reinforce all language arts, art, and penmanship lessons.

■ The children are in charge of cleaning the table tops in the school library, using this daily task for arithmetic practice and health lessons.

Grade Two

■ Each pupil makes up a story, writes it, illustrates it, makes a cover for it, and turns it into a small book. Pages are numbered, perhaps some stories include arithmetic story problems. All of the language-arts skills as well as art lessons are used, and when completed, the pupils give the books to preschoolers and kindergartners, and to the children's section of the local public library.

■ The children are in charge of decorations for sections of the public halls, and expected, monthly to provide a new mural on a special surface near the central office. They are also in charge of twice-a-day sweeping of the school cafeteria area after the kindergarten pupils have cleaned the tables.

Grade Three

■ Once a month the children are taken to a senior housing project, where two children are paired with one adult. The children bring a science project or math game which has been worked on and perfected in the classroom which the 3rd graders share with the elderly. The whole class sings a song for all the residents, and then teach the song to them, all singing together when they finish. Before they leave, each of the children reads a story they have written to one of the adults.

■ The children are in charge of "sweeping" the halls and immediate school grounds for trash, working under the direction of the 6th graders (or custodian if the building does not include 6th graders) to be sure the refuse is prepared for recycling.

Grade Four

- Homework for Wednesday through Sunday is to do singly, or in pairs, or in a small group some community service either for a non-profit agency, or some needy person. Monday, a report is due, either oral or written, about not only what was done, but what doing it has meant.

- Children are in charge of doing errands and delivering messages for any and all administrators and support personnel in the school on a rotating basis. They are in charge of compiling the daily attendance count.

Grade Five

- Youngsters collect money through many different schemes, such as having one week for a read-a-thon, with teachers certifying the appropriate reading level and degree of comprehension. In small groups, responsible for a portion of the collected funds, the 5th graders study all local non-profit agencies, and give their funds to the one (or ones) selected by majority vote of the student group.

- Youngsters are in charge of maintenance and care of all sports equipment in the building and on the playground, working under the direction of a staff person or volunteer students from a nearby secondary school.

Grade Six

■ Every youngster chooses a partner, and each pair chooses a civic organization -- other than the public schools -- such as the police, fire, health clinic, public library, clerk, treasurer, court, etc. both to study for the full school year, and at which to provide some volunteer time and services. Once-a-week reports are required charting use of public monies in the organization each pair is studying. Once a month newsletter is produced describing all activities through lessons in the language arts, using history, geography, science, math, and health lessons.

■ All 6th graders, in groups of three, are responsible for cleanliness and supplies in each of the bathrooms, including those used by both staff and students. Their work is overseen by a member of the building staff or a volunteer student from a nearby secondary school, perhaps an 11th grader planning a co-op in a custodial position.

Grade Seven

■ Once each marking period, in groups of no less than 20, youngsters do a special community service project together. A fall project, for example, putting a public park "to bed" for the winter. Or a fall project to hold a special olympics field day. Maybe a winter project to scrub every piece of woodwork in a local hospital or nursing home. In the spring, perhaps cleanup alongside a local stream or pond or lake.

■ Youngsters do all school grounds maintenance which does not require power tools; in charge of all plantings.

Grade Eight

■ Every youngster is a pen and phone pal to one hospitalized or home-bound child or adult, making personal visits if and when appropriate and convenient. Each contact to be used for the biography the 8th graders are writing about their chosen person, providing information about personal history in context of the history of the times. Biographical "chapters" are to be handed in weekly for combined social studies and English assignments (allowing an oral history when appropriate), and the finished book to be duplicated, one copy given to the subject.

■ All 8th graders are to tutor and/or mentor some younger pupil on a regular basis. A chess player might engage a 3rd grader in this exciting game of logic. An 8th grader who has struggled with spelling, might help a 2nd grader who finds spelling a chore.

Grade Nine

■ In groups of three to five, students should choose a non-profit or civic organization which they "adopt" for the year, working out volunteer assignments in conjunction with job supervisors. Once job assignments are made, the students negotiate with appropriate teachers to present material in conjunction with one of their courses. For example, that group of students who are asked to help design and run a fund campaign for the Civic Theatre

Group, agree with their math teachers how many and what types of financial reports will be acceptable for academic credit.

■ Ninth graders, in pairs, are responsible for the cleaning and care of all public area floors, including front office, halls, library, cafeteria, etc. They are supervised either by school staff, or 12th graders co-opping toward custodial and maintenance jobs.

Grade Ten

■ In small groups, or possibly in class groupings, students devote a school year to studying a local environmental problem, such as water quality, trash disposal, waste management, air pollution, etc. One paper each marking period, done partially as independent study under the direction of a member of the faculty with expertise in the sciences, should deal with the environmental problem and its potential solution. Where possible, the community service study and activity should be integrated with history and English coursework. Also, where possible, information gathered locally should be included in regional and statewide reports on the environmental issues under study. During this year, each student should locate an individual co-op ed assignment to be done during grade 11.

■ Under supervision of school staff or a co-op ed senior, groups of 10th graders should be responsible for light maintenance and repair of all power tools and equipment. All playing and park areas used by the school should be maintained by these young adults.

Grade 11

■ In each student's chosen major interest (e.g. law for a college-bound student; clerking for a job-bound student), a job placement of 20 hours a week, minimum, -- with or without pay -- for one marking period in a non-profit agency or department of government. At least one academic teacher must supervise the work assignment, and portfolio of material required for necessary academic grades and credit.

■ For one marking period, be a tutor, work supervisor, or motivational mentor to a younger student.

Grade 12

■ On a "sandwich" basis (e.g., half days; every other day; one marking period in school and one on-the-job), preferably with pay, hold down a cooperative education job co-jointly supervised by an employer and a teacher. Perhaps working for the town manager, studying and reporting on ways to reduce trash through recycling activities; and simultaneously under the direction of a chemistry teacher working on a special project requiring research in chemistry texts and field research in the town's waste.

■ For a convenient period, be a tutor, work supervisor, or motivational mentor to a younger student.

CHAPTER EIGHT
Who's responsible for the co-op bridge?

Who is responsible? Perhaps I should have dealt with this question sooner in "Chapter One" instead of way back here. But I'm chary of my readers. I know how difficult it is to make radical change, and I thought I better not get you bogged down before getting you fired up.

If the answer was as simple as the question, it would be: "The schools."

But our local public schools are not independent agencies. They get their marching orders from their state constitutions, and are regulated by staffs answerable to their state boards and commissioners of education. In addition, most public schools are union shops for both teachers and support staffs, and their regulations and negotiations play a critical role in how local schools are run, and what types of teaching methods and programs are prevalent.

Then, too, each school is in a school district, and each district has a governing board. In some cases, individual schools have boards as well.

Since all public schools hire college graduates as full-time teachers and administrators, what K-12 public schools are like depends to an enormous extent on what kinds of teachers, principals, and support staff are available, and the major pipeline for new teachers are those colleges and universities with certified teacher-training programs.

Then, too, there are the taxpayers. Individual taxpayers as well as tax-paying businesses. They can cause an issue -- or even a single program not covered by state or union regulations -- to be voted in or voted down.

Parents and politicians both play large roles in school-related decisions; and both sometimes have educational axes to grind.

Therefore, when our schools fail to provide a bridge or transition from school to work, the finger pointing can go round and round in circles, perhaps never coming to rest.

There's an old saw, used sometimes to poke fun at a major political party, "When the _____'s form a firing line, they stand in a circle."

I'm afraid co-op ed has been caught in just such a circle for a long, long time.

I'd like to take it out of this destructive circle. I'd like us to take a fresh new view of the purpose for mandating 10 years (ages 6-16) of schooling for every single child in the United States. And I'd like us to accept a new line of responsibility for giving our children the threefold gifts of citizenship, the bridge to productive employment, and ever-continuing opportunities for higher education.

The force I envision -- that is, that force strong enough to see that all our schools provide co-op ed for every student across this nation -- requires cooperation from two of the largest segments of our national community; the independent (non-profit) sector and our free-enterprise, profit-making businesses and industries.

These, and the various levels of government, are each community's employers. Let every local employer begin offering jobs to all pupils starting in kindergarden and continuing through grade 12. Let every employer make clear to 16-year old school leavers and high school graduates that first-choice jobs go to those who have proven their mettle as volunteers in the non-profit and civic sectors as well as in jobs which fuse academic knowledge with job-skill training in productive employment.

Let every employer of student volunteers, using public service announcement space in all media, tell of the voluntary work of local students, celebrating their activities and concerns, and seeing to it that credit is rendered where credit is due. Do more than keep track of hours: tell of challenges met and conquered; of thoughtfulness beyond the commonplace; of caring greater than the obvious.

Be sure that school trophy spaces are filled with tributes to volunteerism and cooperative education accomplishments.

Promise higher education and full or part-time employment for successful student-workers. Give, if possible, even more attention for a job well done to student-workers than for a game well played to student-athletes.

If you (you employers) ever thought you had no part to play in the bringing-up of our nation's children, you should never think so again. It's only when the academic courses are integrated with the work and service experiences, that the lessons learned are full and complete.

We've all encouraged a toddler to parrot the numbers from one to ten, but we know, and even the toddler knows, that counting without something to count is meaningless. Well, so are all school lessons -- they are of little value until applied.

For the non-profit sector, making place for very young student volunteers, and seeing to it that they grow in personal development, job skills, and sound work attitudes, is a new role for most. But you know you need help; and with a little imaginative planning you can easily see how the meeting of your needs and the meeting of each pupil's needs can be mutually beneficial.

I visited a friend's mother in a very large nursing home for the elderly with a significant number of residents confined to beds and chairs. In a brief chat with the superintendent, I asked if she could think of a job which needed doing she thought could be done by young school pupils. She didn't hesitate: "I have 60 people who need to be fed their main meal at noon each day, and have only 20 people at most who can be spared to do this."

I asked, "Would you send a bus to the local junior high for 40 students each noon hour? And would you make double trays so the students could eat while helping to feed the residents? And then return them to school in time for their next class?" Her answers were: "Yes, yes, and gladly."

That could be the first step. Next might be for the English composition and literature teachers to take advantage of this daily inter-generational experience to guide reading assignments, and to call on the thoughts of the students for fresh reflective writing. Of course, the health classes could well use what the students were learning about the care of the elderly to enhance reading assignments and class discussions.

The student-feeders might well want to have their art work displayed in the rooms of their new friends. And they might well want to add books written, illustrated, and bound by themselves to the nursing-home library.

The Internal Revenue Service will provide tutors for school pupils willing to help the elderly file their income tax returns, and these student-feeders might be given an extra period for two or three days one week in early February to provide this special service for their new friends, learning in the process the purpose of mathematical precision and accurate reading comprehension.

Each student-feeder has a rare primary source at hand each noon with whom to talk over the historic events being discussed and researched for history, government, and social studies classes.

Multiply this nursing home's needs by every human service agency in every village, town, and city. Add all the possible activities children could do to help local, state, and federal civil service workers. And add to those all the possible work-study jobs secondary school students could handle for the many businesses in each community.

89

What does this arithmetic give us? Jobs which help children and young adults learn, and learning which teaches students how to be problem solvers. Also gives us an opportunity to make learners, academic successes, out of a greater number of school students.

This arithmetic also provides a richer and more productive life for our elderly, and all those in need of basic human services. And for the cooperating businesses? The guarantee of a better trained, better educated class of employees.

And it's certainly safe to predict that those wanting to go right on to a four-year liberal arts college will not have been "damaged" by engaging in volunteer service and a term of co-op ed. While we've not got much in the way of empirical evidence on which to base that statement, all anecdotal evidence supports the premise that both work-study and service-learning enhance both academic and job strengths.

Hence, I see a way out of the circle of "who." Who's responsible? Let our nation's employers -- of both volunteers and paid workers -- lead the way out. Let them go to the schools suggesting ways they can provide the vital "hands on" experience so badly needed by fledgling learners.

They can set up new reward systems for students, celebrating jobs well done. They can cite those schools best able to integrate academic coursework with service jobs and co-op ed.

Let the schools in each district be ranked by all employers -- ranked by how well they build the bridges to community service and full-time employment, as well as to higher education. Publish these rankings, celebrate the best in each community, each region, each state, and the nation.

In other words, I'm suggesting that those who will benefit most from better trained and educated high schoolers should take the responsibility for seeing to it that the transition from school to work includes the most suitable cooperative education experience for each individual student.

And I have no hesitancy in predicting that once the bridge is built, not only will it be crossed by competent student-workers, but that school authorities, school boards, education commissioners, and teacher-training institutions will want to be included in both the approach roadways and the bridges themselves. They will change the way they train teachers, supervise teachers, expose students to community service opportunities, and view the implications of work-study which is a fusion of academics and hands-on experience.

Waiting for educationists to change themselves is like "Waiting for Godot." An interesting dialogue; no satisfaction or accomplishment. Ignoring the "forgotten half," is foolhardy. Each young adult who has not completed school, and never held a satisfying job is a walking time bomb -- social dynamite.

Every single economic study tells us that our under-educated and unemployed youth cost us many times more than the cost of four years at an expensive college. For those caught up in the criminal or foster-care system, costs can be three or four times the cost of higher education.

We cannot build enough security fences, hire enough private guards, or own enough attack dogs to keep the "forgotten half" from wanting what every young adult wants: financial independence and a growing sense of self-worth.

It may take longer than the compulsory school years to get some students across the college or co-op ed bridge, but certainly we don't need to leave one of every two students behind. We won't if we begin using bridge experiences to enliven classroom lessons. If, as is suggested in Chapter Seven, kindergarteners can provide local hospitals with folded and decorated napkins, and by so doing the children begin to get a firm grasp on number facts and concepts, then every service organization which could use such napkins needs to begin asking for this service work from the local schools.

Such a request is not selfish; it's good for the doers. And particularly good for the school personnel who know that learning by doing is more powerful than purely didactic teaching, but who, for the moment, have lost their way. They've been too long in the circle of recrimination.

CHAPTER NINE
Caution!

☐ **Put liberal-arts first; co-op ed second.**

☐ **Watch out for, and avoid, service without learning.**

☐ **Don't underestimate student decision-making ability.**

☐ **Eliminate passive learning; replace with active.**

☐ **Isolation out; collaboration in.**

The CED (Committee for Economic Development), in their report <u>Investing in Our Children: Business and the Public Schools</u>, offer the following view of the purpose of schooling:

"Business in general is not interested in narrow vocationalism. In many respects, business believes that the schools in recent years have strayed too far in that direction. For most students, employers would prefer a curriculum that stresses literacy, mathematical skills, and problem-solving skills; one that emphasizes learning how to learn and adapting to change."

David H. Lynn and Dennis Gray, in their commentary on my Grant Commission paper, after citing that paragraph argue: "Those needs and goals are, unquestionably, best met by the liberal arts within a unified and coherent curriculum. And every aspect of a school's program should be focused on meshing with and strengthening that curriculum.

"Specialized programs, therefore, whether in a 'magnet' school stressing the sciences or in a cooperative initiative involving students during their last years in high school, must be seen as viable only to the extent that they ensure a student's mastery of the basic curriculum and build on it."

These colleagues at the Council for Basic Education issue a vital warning: "If tardiness is ignored [by schools], vandalism merely repaired, scholarly achievement not expected or valued, honesty not demanded, discipline not consistent, fair, and predictable, students will learn a view of allowable behavior that is skewed.

"Co-op programs," they continue, "can and should certainly work to reinforce more productive behavior, but here...the role of the co-op is secondary to the larger purpose of the school, not the reverse." They bolster this declaration with the following quotation from Investing in Our Children:

"Such traits as honesty, reliability, self-discipline, cooperativeness, competitiveness, and perseverance are as important to continued scholarship and responsible citizenship as they are essential to success in the workplace. Schools have a responsibility -- and an opportunity -- to help instill these habits."

I used to believe that our schools' problems, while admittedly complex, were mostly curriculum-related, and that by "fixing" the curriculum, we would fix the schools. My first book was based on this premise. But Schools Can Change (Boston: Sterling Institute Press, 1969), went out of print rather quickly, not just because its publisher went out of business in 1970, but because I was wrong.

Not all that wrong; the curriculum is the heart of the scholarship of a school, and scholarship is what schools are all about. Or, it's what they should be all about.

We've got a matrix of responsibility to change, not just the curriculum. And we've got a school purpose to change, or we'll always have a forgotten half. Curriculum is one of the most important functions in the school matrix, but teaching methods must rank nearly as high. And tracking doesn't belong in there at all.

Please don't misunderstand me; don't let my enthusiasm for service-learning and co-op ed lead you astray. I don't think that working is a substitute for studying, no matter how important or how fulfilling the work is.

BUT

To have a teacher of French tell me that she'd love to have her students do community service, but that she needs "every" class period for the lessons or they would "never" complete the course -- particularly in view of the fact her community is close to the French-Canadian border -- is ridiculous. Utterly ridiculous.

Did she teach translation? I asked as though I did not know. "But of course." Well, then, I mused, would it be possible for her on behalf of each of her pupils to locate a native French-speaking pen pal in a local home for the elderly, to begin a correspondence, and to turn in for correction and grading a translation into English of each letter written in French from the pen pal?

Did she teach French songs and dances to her pupils? "But of course." Well then, I mused, wouldn't those native French-speaking elderly richly enjoy hearing and seeing the singers and dancers?

I cannot conceive of any French teacher, whose goal it is to teach French to the pupils in the course, not looking for every opportunity for each pupil to practice that language skill with a native. Never mind the grand lessons which come from bringing joy and enthusiasm to the lonely and discouraged...just the scholarship opportunities alone should have every teacher of every foreign language looking for genuine practice opportunities for every pupil.

Some 10- and 11-year olds taught a similar lesson to their teacher. The pupils in a 5th grade class which had "adopted" a ten-bed nursing home were the first to recognize the rich resource they had. They asked the teacher if they could send a tape recorder and fresh tape to the nursing home and ask the residents, who when they were fifth graders must have known someone who had lived during the Civil War, to tell what they had learned about it.

The students made use of that oral history in their written reports, in turn, sharing those with their nursing-home adoptees.

Messrs. Lynn and Gray are correct: "Every aspect of a school's program should be focused on meshing with and strengthening...curriculum."

Some 14 years ago, John Henry Martin directed a national panel studying "High School and Adolescent Education." The report argued that "...with a few notable exceptions, the vocational shop courses in both comprehensive high schools and vocational centers fail in their stated objectives." This led the panel to endorse work-study and cooperative education programs which they insisted should be directed jointly by "business, industry, and union representatives, as well as teachers and students."

Today, Ted Sizer, founder of the Coalition of Essential Schools, wants such coordination to drive the curriculum -- and for students to take a much more active role in not only determining what they want to learn, but how they want to learn it, and what products they want as a result of their work and study.

He's not having an easy time getting standard educationists to agree with his view of how to structure schools, build curriculum, and broaden teaching and learning experiences. By and large, deans of graduate schools of education and undergraduate heads of departments of education -- just as they ignore service-learning and co-op ed -- pay little or no attention to the coalition's initiatives.

Hard-to-reach and hard-to-teach adolescents are a challenge to us all. We cannot deny them access to citizenship, should not deny them access to a job, and should do everything possible to provide them with a liberal-arts education. Not doing so -- "forgetting" them -- is no way to run a democracy, to build a sound economy, to have a drug-free society, or to live in communities built on trust and understanding.

There's considerable evidence that students respond most positively when given the opportunity to help make decisions which effect them directly. Involving students early in career decisions (or exploration) promotes maturity, excites curiosity, and helps to initiate skill acquisition.

In addition, study after study has proved that the didactic method of teaching -- passive listening by pupils, talking and demonstrating by teachers -- is the least effective for all learners, but close to devastating for all youngsters who are kinetic learners. Yet the estimate is that 90 percent of all schoolteachers more than 90 percent of the time use the didactic method.

Providing all students in all public schools with a better balance between active and passive learning experiences is one key to the reduction of the "at risk" population. In fact there's recently been some feedback which just might help furnish the motivation.

Businesses are beginning to explain to teachers that they expect problems facing employees to be dealt with, not by personnel in isolation, but by small groups of employees working in cooperation with each other. The notion that a group of math students should not work together to solve a problem, but should work in isolation, expecting punishment if they were to attempt to cooperate, is being seriously challenged.

Businesses don't want to hire employees who don't know how to seek help from their fellow workers; or employees who don't share information which would help solve a persistent problem. Co-op ed students learn this the moment they start to work in a job setting.

Research scholars cooperate, writers and editor cooperate, engineers cooperate, -- in fact, it is difficult to think of any profession in which cooperation is not a basic method of operation. Difficult, that is, if one does not recall that almost all elementary schools isolate children in classrooms with single teachers who seldom have any collegial relationship with either fellow teachers or with supervisory personnel.

Or if you do not recall that even at the high school level, learning is broken up into so-called disciplines, and the French I teacher and the English I teacher are given no planning time together, are not expected to reinforce grammar lessons for each other's pupils, and almost never ask their students to learn from each other.

I spent 15 years working for a newspaper. There's just no way a paper can be written and edited without an enormous amount of cooperative teaching and learning. I certainly welcome the fledgling effort of those who are teaching elementary and secondary school teachers how to teach children to work from drafts, and to accept and welcome editorial comments.

Perhaps this movement will grow and develop, and no longer will teachers assign next-to-meaningless compositions, expecting the finished product and the first draft to be one and the same. Should any English composition student co-op in a business based on the publication of the written word, he/she would certainly want the classroom teaching to prepare him/her to work with a succession of editors.

I can recall the struggle each editor at my newspaper had with high school and college interns. Often these were the "top" English comp. students. Those who had had their papers starred and put on bulletin boards since the early grades. Unless their teachers had subjected them to criticism followed by rewrites, these bright students were astounded at the request of an editor that they "do a new lead, drop the second paragraph, pick up three points from wire copy, and do another interview before handing the story in for a second reading."

Let us now imagine a student -- a 1st grader. And let's look in on this student, albeit sketchily, through to grade 12, and a full semester of co-op ed in a local bank. We'll call him "Jim," but she could be Jane.

Jim's a city boy, lives in a rental apartment. He begins learning about work at school by having a daily chore starting in 1st grade. During the primary grades, these chores consist mostly of cleaning and clerking.

Some of the books and stories Jim reads in school and at home are about people doing different jobs; and Jim often helps write stories about work and workers. He writes about his own chores and how he does them. He keeps a work log, noting not only how much time he's spent on a job, but what he's accomplished.

Jim's class "adopts" one wing of a nearby nursing home, and Jim makes a special pal there starting in 1st grade and lasting until 7th. Jim writes stories for his pal; also draws him pictures. Sometimes his pal says he doesn't feel good enough to send a card to a friend, so Jim writes the message and addresses the envelope.

Starting in 3rd grade, Jim's teachers have several of the students play work simulation games where they learn to handle money in retail and marketing situations. Sometimes Jim's homework requires him to interview managers at the stores near his apartment house, to learn what they do and why.

Sometimes he interviews employees at the same stores, and makes oral reports to his class about what he's learned. And all this time, he does a daily work chore at school, keeps on helping out at the nursing home, and is included in several school community service projects.

Starting in the 4th grade, he not only continues to keep a record of his chores and time spent working, but begins writing a journal putting down what he's thinking about what he learns. He adds information about green-up days, the difference between having a "big brother" and being a "big brother," and why he doesn't like fund drives.

Starting in the 6th grade, Jim is encouraged to join in with several other school friends, to choose a community service need, and to design a project to help solve the need. His teachers work with him and his friends, and they decide to put out a neighborhood newspaper, which mostly deals with information about local meetings.

A college student and two high school students offer to help them get started. The high schoolers' help is part of an independent study project, and they get English credit for their work. The college student is a business major, and he wants some practice in how to set up and finance such an organization.

Partly because of Jim's involvement with the local nursing home, and also because many of the other students in on the newspaper project do voluntary service at that and other nursing homes in the area, the paper has one section just for news about the non-profit agencies in the area. And Jim, in an early issue, interviews his special pal and writes a story about the kind of work he did as a banker before he went into the nursing home.

It's Jim who decides to put a <u>Volunteer Help Wanted</u> column in the paper as a favor to all the service agencies in the area.

Jim's high school is a short bus ride away, but he chose this one because they put out a school newspaper, and Jim likes that work. He finds he's getting particularly interested in finance and business, and for history, math, English, and even science courses, he's begun looking at themes in economic terms.

Jim discovers that he really likes math, and offers to work with a team of students who are turning the school district's huge line-item budget into a program budget. Several very experienced bankers and accountants agree to help the students, and Jim finds himself more and more impressed with the broad range of activities possible in banking.

At the same time, since he's still volunteering at the nursing home, he asks the business manager there if he and some of the more advanced math students could help the nursing home with some financial analysis of costs and benefits.

Due to the fact that Jim's high school allows students to co-op in grades 11 and 12; that is, to alternate a week on a job with a week in school, and Jim thinks he might like to do this, he is allowed to "shadow" some of the upper class students in various job locations.

Because of this type of cooperative education schedule, and because the businesses doing the hiring need full-time help, two students fill one job slot, covering for each other for illness, and other absenteeism problems. Jim's choice for grade 11 is in a bank's message center; his other "half" is a girl at his high school.

Jim is one of 24 eleventh graders at his high school working at banks. They have been assigned a 12th grade co-op student, also working at a bank, who serves as their "big sister." She's not the only help they get; every one of the 24 has a designated supervisor at the job site, and must check in with the school's co-op ed coordinator on a regular basis.

But senior co-op students guide 11th grade co-ops, much the same way that senior counselors help junior counselors in summer camp settings.

During the work week, Jim attends a twice-a-week seminar held at the high school which includes a mix of co-ops from all different occupations. Each week they focus on a different aspect of their businesses, and are expected to contribute the research data they have collected. For example, one week Jim is required to determine the promotion flow differential for males and females at his branch bank.

Another week, he's expected to bring a management chart depicting the personnel structure in the bank. Some sessions are held by business representatives, some by union officials, and some by former high school co-op students.

On the three days of the week the seminar is not held, Jim continues to work with the newspaper he helped set up, and once a week meets with his "little brother," a handicapped sixth grader he takes swimming at the Y. Because of this swimming activity, Jim may count his swimming time as part of meeting his physical education requirement.

During the week Jim is in school, his English teacher accepts a paper -- an observation assignment -- detailing what he learned observing a bank clerk for five afternoons in a row. Jim's math teacher is using the construction of the program budget as part of Jim's math assignments, and he and a partner begin working on program costs for the whole intramural athletic program, and then sport by sport. Jim, of course, starts with swimming.

Jim's history teacher assigns a team of students, all co-ops in banks, to study the Federal Reserve System, and how it evolved. They are to make a video presentation at a school assembly as their "finished product."

The summer between Jim's junior and senior years in high school he spends working for a construction company. His family not only expects him to earn enough to buy his own clothes, take care of his entertainment, but to begin to give something for the running of the household.

He decides to co-op for the same construction outfit in the front office, under the direction of the bookkeeper, trying to decide by doing so whether he would rather be in a bank, or in the finance end of a busy company. He continues to attend the twice-a-week seminars taught by the co-op ed counselors, but for the weeks he's in school, he's working with two different small groups on two different independent projects.

When the spring of his senior year comes around, Jim goes to the bank where he did his 11th grade co-op, and they say they would like to have him apply for a job. But they are frank with him; if he doesn't go on to college, he won't be able to hold any professional positions, just those at the clerk level. The construction company also says they would be interested in hiring him full time, and they suggest he work for a while before starting college.

Jim, with the help of one of the officers at the bank, makes out a financial chart; one part showing income and expenditures if he goes to work full time, and the other detailing indebtedness accruing from college tuition. Jim is really eager to move out of the two-room apartment, and he'd like to be able to afford to live on his own.

He's seen enough in his jobs and from his talks for those six years with his special pal in the nursing home to know he's got to get a college education if he ever wants to have a management job. So, he moves in with two other employees at the construction company, works 40 hours a week during the day, and starts night classes at a community college, majoring in business and finance.

BUT

This is all very fanciful. Our "Jim" has been a stalwart lad, never getting into trouble, doing his school, work and service assignments correctly and well. He's guided and directed by dedicated staff at schools and work sites. Lives in a stable, but modest home, etc. etc.

For one "Jim" like that, there will be a dozen students with all kinds of disruptive health, family, work, and academic problems. But coordinating service and jobs with learning don't cause such problems; quite the contrary, all evidence points to a lessening of such disruptions when students are engaged in active instead of passive learning.

In addition, it is estimated that some 60 to 70 percent of all high school students hold down jobs taking up as much as 20 hours a week. But they are almost entirely placed in dead-end jobs. And as they deal with the disruptions in their lives, they move from one entry-level, dead-end job to another, gaining neither strong academic or job skills in the process.

The National Child Labor Committee deserves the final word -- well, not quite final, as there is a wonderful postlude not to be missed. The Committee compared non co-op high school graduates with co-op graduates and concluded:

> "Graduates of co-op programs have a better understanding of the workplace, greater certainty about their career choice, increased work-related competencies, and more experience in the skills involved in searching for a job.
>
> "The distinguishing characteristics of cooperative... education are that the program is jointly planned, structured, and supervised."

Postlude
by John R. Coleman

She just cannot be that right. There must be other reasons than those in Cynthia Parsons's book on why cooperative education is not more widely prevalent and praised in our schools today.

Maybe the problem is that...

...if business leaders are so competent to play meaningful roles in bringing joint educational efforts into the schools, their diplomas would all show a minimum of 12 undergraduate or graduate credits in a state-certified School of Education.

...if the Founding Fathers wanted us to go down the co-op road nationally, they would have broken their silence on education in the U. S. Constitution and the Bill of Rights to endorse this one path to progress.

...if God meant us to expose our young ones to such ways of schooling, Jesus would not have ended his sentence with just "Suffer the little children to come unto me, and forbid them not;" he would have added, "to learn even as they do."

How do you answer those arguments, Cynthia Parsons? Do you mean to have us ignore the educational establishment, the Founding Fathers, and God all at the same time? Where then is your certainty rooted?

Fifty years ago, the historian Arnold Toynbee wrote that "there is no one alive today who knows enough to say with confidence whether one religion has been greater than all the others." (Ah, come back and say it in 1990, Professor Toynbee.) That may also be true for education of the young.

And yet...

And yet...

And yet some part of me persists in believing that the case for The Co-op Bridge is compelling. So compelling that I can only shake my head in dismay and wipe my tears in grief (admittedly, my friends say I cry easily) that we have so long ignored, or at a minimum played down, those arguments in our schools.

Most of my life's work has been in education, but only at the college level. The closest I've come to open advocacy of what Cynthia Parsons is writing about here resulted in two of my three major defeats as president of a small liberal arts college: I could neither persuade my own department (economics) to include some elements of accounting in the curriculum, nor persuade the entire faculty to require all students coming to us directly from high school to take a minimum of one semester off to do something else for a while.

The case for accounting was that it could be useful in the work world afterwards and that, properly taught, it could be a fruitful way of organizing some data and some concepts for problem-solving ends. The case for time away was that the students with wider experience of the world around -- almost any experience -- were both more directed and more contributing members in class discussions on their return.

110

(A loose end: the third of those defeats in the presidency was the effort to make the college co-educational. But that defeat became victory soon after I left the scene, and now folks there ask, "What was the fight all about?" I should live so long as to see the other defeats turn out so well.)

Those encounters with resistance to change do not dim my affection and my respect for educators who, day after day, go into classrooms to advance learning in the young and in themselves. And yet the same encounters only deepen my stubborn conviction that for much too long we have needlessly narrowed the definition of what constitutes schooling and education in our society.

The case here, with telling examples, is one for breaking out of that mold. Early on. It is the case for treating so much more that surrounds our children as integral parts of the process of their learning to live more fully and work more effectively. That in turn, is the case for viewing the separate contributors to education -- the teachers with certificates, the employers with market experience, the parents with concerns and hopes, the critics with agendas -- as distinctive but interdependent players in the growth story.

The root problem with Cynthia Parsons's case for The Co-op Bridge, I suspect, are fear in some quarters and arrogance in others. Fear may exist among the educators that joint efforts with outsiders in defining and implementing the school agenda will decrease their own worth. Arrogance may rule among those who, fresh from success experiences in business, assume that they hold the answers to the educators' prayers. What teacher is really ready to say, "I can use help from those for whom my students will eventually work, in shaping the school experience?" What business leader is really ready to admit, "I need to recognize that my contribution to today's schools is, at best, only a supplement to what the teachers know and do each day?"

We probably pay a high price for giving too little credit to teachers for what they do and too much credit to business leaders for what they do. If our schools are as bad as those outside them complain, we could scarcely have as many people functioning so well and happily both on and off their jobs as we do. If our businesses are as well run as their defenders claim, we could scarcely be facing the current world-wide challenges to our workplace leadership and the glaring needs to think far beyond today's profits to tomorrow's. Building bridges together might just result in more pride where it is most needed, and more humility where that is needed.

The Parsons case for co-op bridges is advanced in the name of our children, and our grandchildren. If these bridges were built as she envisions and illustrates them, the crossovers and adventures beyond could bring growth far beyond those young people. Educators and employers together could grow in ways that they can scarcely dream of now. Grow in self-confidence. Grow in sense of self-worth. Grow in the joy of interdependence alongside the pride of independence.

So, why don't we get on with more co-op education?

No one need claim this would lead to solutions for all the ills that beset us daily. It is enough that it could lead to making the schools more important, relevant, and lasting, and making the people in them, full-time and part-time, more contributing, whole and fun to be with.

That should be case enough. But will it be? Watch. Wait. And pray a lot.

---

1. John R. Coleman, author of Blue Collar Journal (1974) and other books, is the former president of the Edna McConnell Clark Foundation in New York and Haverford College in Pennsylvania. He is presently the owner/breakfast chef of the Inn at Long Last in Chester, Vermont.

Also by Cynthia Parsons:

Teacherly wisdom of the impassioned, no-nonsense kind. Here is intellectual rigor, as well as a personal element.
—The Kirkus Reviews

Seeds: Some Good Ways To Improve Our Schools

From an author superbly qualified, here are more than 180 ways in which teachers and parents can help our youth to a dramatically improved education—without spending large amounts of additional money. ... Ideas that can be implemented right now.

"Parsons offers specific, challenging suggestions for improving every aspect of public schooling—the ethos, the principals, the teachers, discipline, the curriculum, the budget, the parents—within a revised structure. Parsons wants the schools to consider the whole needs of the child and provide a classical education."—*The Kirkus Reviews.*

ISBN 0-88007-148-6, hard cover, 6x9, 220pp., $15.95

Order from: Woodbridge Press, Box 6189,
Santa Barbara, California 93160   1(800)963-0540

SerVermont and the U.S.A.

Cynthia Parsons, coordinator of Vermont's statewide student community service initiative, calls this her service-learning recipe book. In the most practical ways, it tells both how to and why to incorporate service in the school curriculum. K-12. $6.

What'll You Have?

Fifty+ non-alcoholic drink recipes in an attractive spiral-bound paperback. Excellent for use by MADD and SADD chapters (bulk orders for resale). Just right for teen parties. Beautiful calligraphy, and bright cover for gift-giving. $5.

Order the above two books from:

Vermont Schoolhouse Press, Box 516, Chester, VT 05143